OF CATERPILLARS, CATS AND CATTLE

Of Caterpillars, Cats a... ...of poems about animals ...ic pets, night creatures, bi...

Familiar names abound i... ...in this anthology – Wal... ...ed Lord Tennyson and Ted ...on but a few – as well as those poets perhaps not so well known – Phoebe Hesketh, Frances Cornford and Norman MacCaig.

There are poems covering every sphere of the animal world – birth, death, the hunter and the hunted, the adored pet, creatures of the town, country and farm, creatures of the night.

Enhanced by William Geldart's exquisite drawings, *Of Caterpillars, Cats and Cattle* offers a wide collection of poems which make a fascinating and very pleasurable read.

Anne Harvey has had a passion for poetry since childhood, and poetry and drama are an important part of her life. As well as teaching drama and examining for the Poetry Society, she organizes a group of actors who perform programmes of poetry and prose, and she also edits books, writes for the press and broadcasts on radio. *Poets in Hand*, her anthology of the work of five contemporary poets, is also published in Puffin.

Another collection from Anne Harvey:

POETS IN HAND A Puffin Quintet

OF CATERPILLARS, CATS AND CATTLE

CHOSEN BY ANNE HARVEY
Illustrated by William Geldart

PUFFIN BOOKS

For Gervase

'Animals are such agreeable friends – they ask no
questions, they pass no criticisms' – George Eliot

PUFFIN BOOKS

Published by the Penguin Group
27 Wrights Lane, London w8 5tz, England
Viking Penguin Inc., 40 West 23rd Street, New York, New York 10010, USA.
Penguin Books Australia Ltd, Ringwood, Victoria, Australia
Penguin Books Canada Limited, 2801 John Street, Markham, Ontario, Canada L3R 1B4
Penguin Books (NZ) Ltd, 182–190 Wairau Road, Auckland 10, New Zealand

Penguin Books Ltd, Registered Offices: Harmondsworth, Middlesex, England

This selection first published by Viking Kestrel 1987
Published in Puffin Books 1988
3 5 7 9 10 8 6 4 2

Printed in Great Britain by
Richard Clay Ltd, Bungay, Suffolk
Filmset in Sabon

Contents

VARIOUS GOOD FRIENDS

AND THE SONG OF A BIRD

OF ALL THE TREASURES THAT WERE MINE

NIGHT'S LIVING THINGS

EARTH'S IMMEASURABLE
SURPRISE

Lark

Hear
That lark
Bold and clear
Far over the park
Rising slowly into the sky,
Joy of morning in his throat,
Until he becomes a dot on high,
A distant speck of sound, a throbbing note,
Companion of the noonday sun, nearly a thousand feet
Above the rooftops, and there he hovers in the haze,
The air his shining kingdom and the clouds his chosen seat.
And then at last contented with his songs of praise,
He drops to earth as if on failing wings;
Before on quiet ground he gently touches down.
I'll not forget the song he sings
Over the houses of the town;
Though I watch him disappear,
Still in the dark,
Bold and clear
That lark
Hear.

LEONARD CLARK

The Cockerel Proclaims

I am proud of my pride.
I open the doors of morning.
I shout the trees awake,
Circle your towns with a high
Magnificent, self-controlled cry.

One by one I snuff out the stars
And I am the first colours,
A reminder of the rainbow,
A singer shaming your small
Complaining voices. I'm tall

And proud of my flaring height.
I am the sun's true herald.
I wind up the small birds' voices,
And tell you it's worth getting up
As I lock the doors of the night.

ELIZABETH JENNINGS

Cock-crow

Out of the wood of thoughts that grows by night
To be cut down by the sharp axe of light, –
Out of the night, two cocks together crow,
Cleaving the darkness with a silver blow;
And bright before my eyes twin trumpeters stand,
Heralds of splendour, one at either hand,
Each facing each as in a coat of arms:
The milkers lace their boots up at the farms.

EDWARD THOMAS

Winter Ducks

Small in the shrink of winter, dark of the frost and chill,
Dawnlight beyond my window sill,
I lace the morning stiffly on my feet,
Print bootsteps down the snowy hill to meet
My ducks all waiting where the long black night
Has iced the pond around them. With a spade
I break the water clear; the hole I made
Restores their world to quacking rhyme and reason –
Tails up, they duck the lowering, grey-skied season,
Heads down, they listen to the still-warm song
Of silted leaves and summer, when the days were long.

RUSSELL HOBAN

Early Waking

'Does a bird rejoice like me
  In this earth-fresh dawn?'

'Dearest, on a silvery tree
  He achieves an ecstasy,
  You, in bed, a yawn.'

FRANCES CORNFORD

Bird at Dawn

What I saw was just one eye
In the dawn as I was going:
A bird can carry all the sky
In that little button glowing.

Never in my life I went
So deep into the firmament.

He was standing on a tree,
All in blossom overflowing,
And he purposely looked hard at me,
At first, as if to question merrily:
'Where are you going?'
But next some far more serious thing to say:
I could not answer, could not look away.

Oh, that hard, round, and so distracting eye:
Little mirror of all the sky!
And then the after-song another tree
Held, and sent radiating back to me.

If no man had invented human word,
And a bird-song had been
The only way to utter what we mean,
What would we men have heard,
What understood, what seen,
Between the trills and pauses, in between
The singing and the silence of a bird?

HAROLD MONRO

The Cat Returns

On cushioned pins the cat returns soft-foot,
Coincident with milk, playing her part.
It has been a long night, but pleasurable
In the various ways that make a cat's life full.

Discover her here, at the house she agrees to visit
But does not need; a familiar, an exquisite.
Should this door ever be barred to her, there are more:
The cat is rare that died for want of a door.

Within the house are two who wanted a child,
Whose lives were voids which the cat's coming filled.

Another day of adoration dawns;
The sun slants into the porch, where the cat yawns,
Patiently awaits their passionate adjectives.

History reiterates such hopeless loves.

ERIC MILLWARD

The First Day

The spotted fawn
awoke in small leaf-spotted suns
tattooing him with coins where he lay
beside his mother's warmth the first day
that gave him light,
the day that played him tunes
in water-music twinking over stones
and leaf-edged undertones,
the day he learned the feel
of dew on grass
cool, cool, and wet,
of sun that steals the dew with sudden heat,
and heard the fret
in wind turned willow leaves and wrinkled pool,
the day that filled his lungs with pollened wind
and smell of bracken, earth, and dell-deep moss,

the day he came to know
sharp hunger and the flow
of milk to comfort his small emptiness,
the strangeness of his legs,
the bulwark of his mother's side,
the solace of her pink tongue's first caress,
her snow-soft belly for his sheltering,
the rhythm of his needs
for movement and for rest,
for food and warmth and nest
of flattened grass to fold himself in sleep.

PHOEBE HESKETH

Birth of the Foal

As May was opening the rosebuds,
elder and lilac beginning to bloom,
it was time for the mare to foal.
She'd rest herself, or hobble lazily

after the boy who sang as he led her
to pasture, wading through the meadowflowers.
They wandered back at dusk, bone-tired,
the moon perched on a blue shoulder of sky.

Then the mare lay down,
sweating and trembling, on her straw in the stable.
The drowsy, heavy-bellied cows
surrounded her, waiting, watching, snuffing.

Later, when even the hay slept
and the shaft of the Plough pointed south,
the foal was born. Hours the mare
spent licking the foal with its glue-blind eyes.

And the foal slept at her side,
a heap of feathers ripped from a bed.
Straw never spread as soft as this.
Milk or snow never slept like a foal.

Dawn bounced up in a bright red hat,
waved at the world and skipped away.
Up staggered the foal,
its hooves were jelly-knots of foam.

Then day sniffed with its blue nose
through the open stable window, and found them –
the foal nuzzling its mother,
velvet fumbling for her milk.

Then all the trees were talking at once,
chickens scrabbled in the yard,
like golden flowers
envy withered the last stars.

FERENC JUHÁSZ
(translated by David Wevill)

Spring Song

On the grassy banks
Lambkins at their pranks;
Woolly sisters, woolly brothers,
   Jumping off their feet,
While their woolly mothers
   Watch by them and bleat.

CHRISTINA ROSSETTI

First Sight

Lambs that learn to walk in snow
When their bleating clouds the air
Meet a vast unwelcome, know
Nothing but a sunless glare.
Newly stumbling to and fro
All they find, outside the fold,
Is a wretched width of cold.

As they wait beside the ewe,
Her fleeces wetly caked, there lies
Hidden round them, waiting too,
Earth's immeasurable surprise.
They could not grasp it if they knew,
What so soon will wake and grow
Utterly unlike the snow.

PHILIP LARKIN

A Child's Voice

On winter nights shepherd and I
   Down to the lambing-shed would go;
Rain round our swinging lamp did fly
   Like shining flakes of snow.

There on a nail our lamp we hung,
   And O it was beyond belief
To see those ewes lick with hot tongue
   The limp wet lambs to life.

A week gone and sun shining warm
   It was as good as gold to hear
Those new-born voices round the farm
   Cry shivering and clear.

Where was a prouder man than I
   Who knew the night those lambs were born,
Watching them leap two feet on high
   And stamp the ground in scorn?

Gone sheep and shed and lighted rain
   And blue March morning; yet today
A small voice crying brings again
   Those lambs leaping at play.

ANDREW YOUNG

Twins

Born in the spring at dead of frosty night,
The moon on cowshed thatch and sleeping house.
Thin cries in darkness, with the lamp's small light
Falling on upturned pail, sharp watching mouse.

A few days old to stand on glassy feet,
Nuzzling together in the littered hay,
Soft liquid eyes at peace, bleat after bleat,
They tug at milky udders all the day.

Let loose at last from smells of raftered home,
Inherit fields of grass and pasture flowers,
A continent of green in which to roam,
Companions of the dawn and twilight showers.

We see them grazing from behind the fence,
And wonder why such frisky calves must grow
To dawdling cows, so stolid and immense,
Who only knew the world a year ago.

LEONARD CLARK

from *Baby Tortoise*

You know what it is to be born alone
Baby tortoise!

The first day to heave your feet little by little from the shell,
Not yet awake,
And remain lapsed on earth,
Not quite alive.

A tiny, fragile, half-animate bean.

To open your tiny beak-mouth, that looks as if it would
    never open,
Like some iron door;
To lift the upper hawk-beak from the lower base
And reach your skinny little neck
And take your first bite at some dim bit of herbage,
Alone, small insect,
Tiny bright-eye,
Slow one.

You draw your head forwards slowly, from your little
    wimple
And set forward, slow-dragging, on your four-pinned toes,
Rowing slowly forward.

Whither away, small bird?
Rather like a baby working its limbs,
Except that you make slow, ageless progress
And a baby makes none.

The touch of sun excites you,
And the long ages, and the lingering chill
Makes you pause to yawn,
Opening your impervious mouth,
Suddenly beak-shaped, and very wide, like some suddenly
    gaping pincers;
Soft red tongue and hard thin gums,
Then close the wedge of your little mountain front,
Your face, baby tortoise.

Do you wonder at the world as slowly you turn your head in
    its wimple
And look with laconic, black eyes?
Or is sleep coming over you again,
The non-life?

You are so hard to wake.

Over the garden earth,
Small bird,
Over the edge of all things.
Traveller,
With your tail tucked a little on one side
Like a gentleman in a long-skirted coat.

All life carried on your shoulder,
Invincible fore-runner.

D. H. LAWRENCE

The Old Dog

What does the old dog say?
Well, here's another day
   To sit in the sun.
And when my master's up,
I'll skip around like a pup,
   And we'll go for a run.
But now, I'll lift my head
Out of my warm bed
   To greet the dawn,
Sigh gently, and slowly turn,
Slowly lie down again,
And softly yawn.

All night I've kept an eye
Open protectingly
   In case of danger.
If anything had gone wrong
I would have raised my strong
   Voice in anger.
But all was safe and still.
The sun's come over the hill,
   No need for warning.
When he comes down the stair
I shall be waiting there
To say Good Morning.

LESLIE NORRIS

THROUGH MY LENS

Magic

Through my lens, this greenfly on a rose-leaf
Becomes in an eye-wink a terrifying monster
Crouching upon the dark-green leathery surface:
Beside him shines a bright round bubble of dew.
How odd, how fearful the world must look to him
As he stares through HIS lens! He sees my face
(Forehead and curving nose and one huge eye
Looming down coldly at him, prying and peering);
My cat, green-tiger-striped with shadows; and that lizard,
A sliding pterodactyl, as it passes
Through the tall, tangled forest of the grasses.

CLIVE SANSOM

Earth-worm

                    Do
                  you
              squirm
        when
you
see
an earth-worm?
  I never
    do squirm
      because I think
        a big fat worm
          is really rather clever
            the way it can shrink
                    and go
                    so small
                  without
                  a sound
                  into the ground.

            And then
            what about
            all
            that
          work it does
        and no oxygen
          or miner's hat?
        Marvellous
            you have to admit,
              even if you don't like fat
              pink worms a bit,
            how with that
                  thin
                slippery skin
              it makes its way

32

day after day
through the soil,
such honest toil.
And don't forget
the dirt
it eats, I bet
you wouldn't like to come out
at night to squirt
it all over the place
with no eyes in your face:
I doubt
too if you know
an earth-worm is deaf, but
it can hear YOU go
to and fro
even if you cut
it in half.
So
do not laugh
or squirm
again
when
you
suddenly
see
a worm.

LEONARD CLARK

34

Snail

Snail upon the wall,
Have you got at all
Anything to tell
About your shell?

Only this, my child –
When the wind is wild,
Or when the sun is hot,
It's all I've got.

JOHN DRINKWATER

The Snail

To grass, or leaf, or fruit, or wall
The snail sticks fast, nor fears to fall,
As if he grew there, house and all,
                              together.

Within that house secure he hides
When danger imminent betides,
Or storms, or other harms besides
                              of weather.

Give but his horns the slightest touch,
His self-collecting power is such,
He shrinks into his house with much
                              displeasure.

Where'er he dwells, he dwells alone,
Except himself, has chattels none,
Well satisfied to be his own
                              whole treasure.

Thus, hermit-like, his life he leads,
Nor partner of his banquet needs,
And if he meets one, only feeds
                              the faster.

Who seeks him must be worse than blind,
(He and his house are so combined)
If finding it he fails to find
                              its master.

WILLIAM COWPER
(translated from the Latin of Vincent Bourne)

The Caterpillar

Brown and furry
Caterpillar in a hurry;
Take your walk
To the shady leaf or stalk.

May no toad spy you,
May the little birds pass by you;
Spin and die,
To live again a butterfly.

CHRISTINA ROSSETTI

The Spider

The Spider holds a Silver Ball
In unperceived Hands –
And dancing softly to Himself
His yarn of Pearl – unwinds –

He plies from Nought to Nought –
In unsubstantial Trade –
Supplants our Tapestries with His –
In half the period –
An Hour to rear supreme
His continents of Light –
Then dangle from the Housewife's Broom –
His Boundaries – forgot –

EMILY DICKINSON

Caterpillar

How soft a Caterpillar steps –
I find one on my Hand
From such a velvet world it comes
Such plushes at command
Its soundless travels just arrest
My slow-terrestrial eye
Intent upon its own career
What use has it for me –

EMILY DICKINSON

The Saffron Butterfly

Out of its dark cocoon,
Like a blossom breaking earth
A saffron winged butterfly
Came to its April birth,
Fluttered by banks of primroses:
I could not tell, not I,
If yellow butterflies starred the hedge,
Or a flower flew in the sky.

TERESA HOOLEY

The Butterfly in Church

Butterfly, butterfly, why come you here?
    This is no place for you;
Go, sip the honey-drop sweet and clear,
Or bathe in the morning dew.

This is the place to think of heaven,
    This is the place to pray:
You have no sins to be forgiven –
    Butterfly, go away!

WILLIAM COWPER

The Cabbage White Butterfly

I look like a flower you could pick. My delicate wings
Flutter over the cabbages. I don't make
Any noise ever. I'm among silent things.
    Also I easily break.

I have seen the nets in your hands. At first I thought
A cloud had come down but then I noticed you
With your large pink hand and arm. I was nearly caught
    But fortunately I flew

Away in time, hid while you searched, then took
To the sky, was out of your reach. Like a nameless flower
I tried to appear. Can't you be happy to look?
    Must you possess with your power?

ELIZABETH JENNINGS

Butterfly

The Butterfly upon the Sky,
That doesn't know its Name
And hasn't any tax to pay
And hasn't any Home
Is just as high as you and I,
And higher, I believe,
So soar away and never sigh
And that's the way to grieve –

EMILY DICKINSON

This Loafer

In a sun-crazed orchard
Busy with blossomings
This loafer, unaware of
What toil or weather brings,
Lumpish sleeps – a chrysalis
Waiting, no doubt, for wings.

And when he does get active,
It's not for business, – no
Bee-lines to thyme or heather,
No earnest to-and-fro
Of thrushes: pure caprice tells him
Where and how to go.

All he can ever do
Is to be entrancing,
So that a child may think,
Upon a chalk-blue chancing,
'Today was special. I met
A piece of the sky dancing.'

CECIL DAY LEWIS

Three Butterflies

Flat on my back
beneath the freckling sun,
three butterflies sail around me,
and very gently, one
settles on my burning face,
folding his dusty wings,
as if he liked the place;
and one hovers a little while
before he decides to land
with cool and delicate feet

upon the thumb of my right hand,
but soon changes his mind, and does not stay
to keep me company, skimming soundlessly away
into the flowers and trees:
and one goes on flitting around
my head at perfect ease,
and will not be my guest.

But how glad I am
that two of them made me
their resting place a minute or so,
believing I was a flower or tree.

LEONARD CLARK

Bee

Bee! I'm expecting you!
Was saying Yesterday
To Somebody you know
That you were due –

The Frogs got home last Week –
Are settled and at work –
Birds, mostly back –
The Clover warm and thick –

You'll get my Letter by
The seventeenth; Reply
Or better, be with me –
Yours, Fly.

EMILY DICKINSON

'Wild Bees had Built . . .'

Wild bees had built, while we had been from home,
A nest inside of the big old-fashioned lock
Of the cottage door; and choked it so with wax
The key wouldn't turn in the wards; and we'd to climb
Into our home across the window-sill.
They must have started as soon as we'd turned our backs,
And set about their labour with right good will,
To have made themselves so secure in the nest, and block
The wards so badly in so short a time:
For they'd even started filling the honeycomb.

Yet, as we entered our little house once more,
It seemed to us not only the wild bees
Had been at work: for we found in each room a store
Of honeyed delight and golden memories.

W. W. GIBSON

Bumble Bee

I am a bumble bee,
think kindly thoughts of me,
I filled my summer mornings
        with my humming.

Now days are growing short
and I suppose I ought
to stop this evening mumble
        in the clover;

but when I think it's done,
the hum goes on and on,
for no-one will believe
        that winter's coming;

when stillness should begin,
small songs keep dropping in
like raindrops from the trees
        when rain is over.

N. M. BODECKER

Bee

I buzz, I buzz, I buzz
because I am a Bee.
I never rest
in my own nest
except when I've
filled up a hive
with excelicious Honey.
From West Ealing
to Darjeeling
no other creature can
produce one jot
or tiny spot
of my divine confection:
no, not for love
or health or wealth
no, sir, not even for money,

can any factory
make satisfactory
natural Norfolk honey.
From this you see
that I, the Bee,
by natural selection
am cleverer than
machines or man
and very near
    perfection.

GEORGE BARKER

The Wasp

When the ripe pears droop heavily,
The yellow wasp hums loud and long
His hot and drowsy summer song.
A yellow flame he seems to be,
When darting suddenly from high
He lights where fallen peaches lie.

Yellow and black – this tiny thing's
A tiger soul on elfin wings.

WILLIAM SHARP

A Country Matter

Out on some nature ramble with the school
I found a hole in the ground tangled with grass
And kicked it – kicked it over again to feel
The earth all round my foot. It was a wasps' nest.
They rose in droning clouds, my head was wasps,
Hands in front of my eyes I stumbled down
The hill, myself a frantic hill of wasps –
One, cleaving to my temple, drilled right in.

My cries, they told me, could have been heard for miles,
But no one came. My fellow-pupils knew
Too well what lumps came up from red-hot weals,
And teachers felt they weren't paid to rescue
Boys from self-inflicted wounds. I ran
Blindly off course, crashed down into the wood,
Splashed across the beck, then up stream bellowing,
Shaking wasps off like confetti as I went.

47

The last one still to my temple clung, and stung
Again and again, digging in his hot lance.
I took him gently between my finger and thumb
And cast him against the air. He circled once
Glancing into the sun, then zoomed away.
There may be a moral here, though not for me;
But that is why, I think, I dream in this way,
Recalling things that nobody else would see.

PHILIP HOBSBAUM

The Ladybird

Ladybird! Ladybird! Where art thou gone?
Ere the daisy was open or the rose it was spread
On the cabbage flower early thy scarlet wings shone,
I saw thee creep off to the tulip's bed.
Ladybird! Ladybird! Where art thou flown?
Thou wert here in the morning before the sun shone.

Just now up the bole o' the damson tree
You passed the gold lichen and got to the grey –
Ladybird! Ladybird! Where can you be?
You climb up the tulips and then fly away.
You crept up the flowers while I plucked them just now
And crept to the top and then flew from the flowers.
O sleep not so high as the damson tree bough,
But come from the dew i' the eldern tree bower.

Here's lavender trees that would hide a lone mouse
And lavender cotton wi' buttons o' gold,
And bushes o' lad's love as dry as a house,
Here's red pinks and daisies so sweet to behold.

Ladybird! Ladybird! Come to thy nest,
Thy gold bed's i' the rose o' the sweetbrier tree,
Wi' rose-coloured curtains to pleasure thee best;
Come, Ladybird, back to thy garden and me.

JOHN CLARE

A Dragonfly

When the heat of the summer
Made drowsy the land,
A dragonfly came
And sat on my hand,
With its blue jointed body,
And wings like spun glass
It lit on my fingers
As though they were grass.

ELEANOR FARJEON

Second Birth

Today I saw the Dragon Fly
Come from the wells where he did lie;
An inner impulse rent the veil
Of his old husk: from head to tail
Came out clear plates of sapphire mail.
He dried his wings – like gauze they grew
Through crofts and pastures wet with dew
A living flash of light he flew.

ALFRED LORD TENNYSON

from *The Fly*

Little Fly,
Thy summer's play
My thoughtless hand
Has brush'd away.

Am not I
A fly like thee?
Or art not thou
A man like me?

For I dance,
And drink, and sing,
Till some blind hand
Shall brush my wing.

WILLIAM BLAKE

Seven Flies

Each autumn in the kitchen
A fly remains. The same?
How can we tell? Except
It seems to grow more tame.

If you're a house-fly
Then I wonder why
You bang on the glass
That keeps you from grass.

You know by my flapping hand I hate your flight;
So why do you want to kiss me in the night?

Fly, who's been very naughty on my dough-
Nut, why do I push the window, let you go?

Fly in the milk, I spoon you out alive
And grieve you're too bedraggled to survive.

Still fly against the wall – it is as if
I stood asleep upon an upright cliff.

A fly on the kitchen pane –
Surely that fly of old!
With cunning suddenness
I push the window out
And as quickly shut it again;
The fly still on the glass
But on the outside now.
Unmoving, sulking, it stays,
Its diamond eyes upon
Sugar and cake and him
Who plays dirty tricks on flies.

ROY FULLER

Simply a Slug

Stalks, lovely stalks.

Through succulent slime
Pierce petals, and leaves
As large as elephant ears.

A non-discriminating tongue.

Shoots, lovely shoots.

Humping along the damp,
Tanking-out luminous trails,
That my eye
Sips in the sun.

There cruised the thug of the underworld.

RONA M. CAMPBELL

VARIOUS GOOD FRIENDS

Happy Calf

Mother is worried, her low, short moos
Question what's going on. But her calf
Is quite happy, resting on his elbows,
With his wrists folded under, and his precious hind legs
Brought up beside him, his little hooves
Of hardly-used yellow-soled black.
She looms up, to reassure him with heavy lickings.
He wishes she'd go away. He's meditating
Black as a mole and as velvety,
With a white face-mask, and a pink parting,
With black tear-patches, but long
Glamorous white eyelashes. A mild narrowing
Of his eyes, as he lies, testing each breath
For its peculiar flavour of being alive.

Such a pink muzzle, but a black dap
Where he just touched his mother's blackness
With a tentative sniff. He is all quiet
While his mother worries to and fro, grazes a little,
Then looks back, a shapely mass
Against the South sky and the low frieze of hills,
And moos questioning warning. He just stays,
Head slightly tilted, in the mild illness
Of being quite contented, and patient
With all the busyness inside him, the growing
Getting under way. The wind from the North
Marching the high silvery floor of clouds
Trembles the grass-stalks near him. His head wobbles
Infinitesimally in the pulse of his life.
A buttercup leans on his velvet hip.
He folds his head back little by breathed little
Till it rests on his shoulder, his nose on his ankle,
And he sleeps. Only his ears stay awake.

TED HUGHES

The Calf

You may have seen, in road or street,
    At times, when passing by,
A creature with bewildered bleat
Behind a milcher's tail, whose feet
    Went pit-pat. That was I.

Whether we are of Devon kind,
    Shorthorns or Herefords,
We are in general of one mind
That in the human race we find
    Our masters and our lords.

When grown-up (if they let me live)
   And in a dairy-home,
I may less wonder and misgive
Than now, and get contemplative,
   And never wish to roam.

And in some fair stream, taking sips,
   May stand through summer noons,
With water dribbling from my lips
And rising halfway to my hips,
   And babbling pleasant tunes.

THOMAS HARDY

To a Cow

They took your calf away last night,
So that is why you moo
And all the beasts in sympathy
Mourn from the field with you!

Commiseration flows from me
It flows from every part
As lying still I hear that low
From out your bovine heart.

Maternal anguish racks your frame
And yet you cannot weep,
Just bellow sadly to the stars –
But please, I want some sleep.

M. JAMES

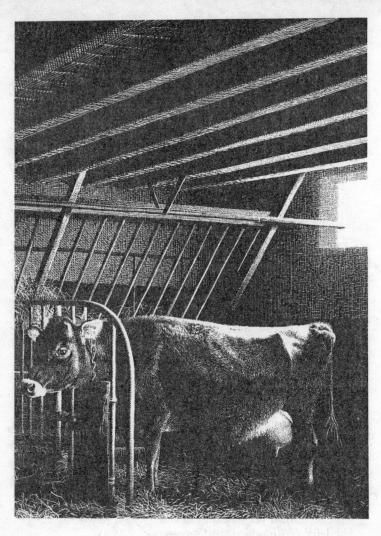

Country Idyll

Deep in the stable tied with rope,
The cow has neither dignity nor hope.

With ugly, puzzled, hot despair
  She needs the calf that is not there,
And mourns and mourns him to unheeding air.

  But if the sleeping farmer hears,
  He pulls the blanket higher round his ears.

FRANCES CORNFORD

The Gracious and
the Gentle Thing

The three young heifers were at Summer supper
In the cowpen munching new-mown hay,
Their eyes suffused with sweetness of red clover,
It was no time to pass the time of day.
Their chins went side to side, their cheeks were bulging
Indecorously, and they were eating more;
I was a stranger, I had no introduction,
They had never laid eyes on me before.

Yet when I patted each young lady's sleekness,
Each young lady's lips grew bland and still,
She left the hay that sweetened the whole evening
And beamed on me with eyes deep with good will.
She kissed my hand where it lay on the fence-rail
And breathed her sweetness in my smiling face;
She left her supper, turned her slender beauty
Instantly to practice of good grace.

I stood there below the azure evening
With miles of tender thrushes all around
And thought how up and down the land I never
So natural a courtesy had found
As this night in a barnyard with three heifers.
The gracious and the gentle thing to do,
With never any lesson in good manners,
These innocent and courteous creatures knew.

ROBERT P. TRISTRAM COFFIN

The Lost Heifer

When the black herds of the rain were grazing
In the gap of the pure cold wind
And the watery haze of the hazel
Brought her into my mind,
I thought of the last honey by the water
That no hive can find.

Brightness was drenching through the branches
When she wandered again,
Turning the silver out of dark grasses
Where the skylark had lain,
And her voice coming softly over the meadow
Was the mist becoming rain.

AUSTIN CLARKE

A Farmer's Boy

They strolled down the lane together,
The sky was studded with stars –
They reached the gate in silence
And he lifted down the bars –
She neither smiled nor thanked him
Because she knew not how;
For he was just a farmer's boy
And she was a Jersey Cow.

ANON.

Lamb

I am the Lamb that whickers
    out of a cloud of dreams
I am the changeling of spring places
    and fields and freshest streams
I am white as Winter was
    and as Love seems.

I jump up into the bright air
    of the April day
so that to me the world will seem
    one moment far away
and then I can leap back on it
    as it goes on its way.

I am the Lamb, the Lamb of Love,
    as holy as the child.
I am the lost black lamb on whom
    the Morning Shepherd smiled.
I lie down with the Lion and
    we slumber in the wild.

GEORGE BARKER

Sheep

There have been times I have been a sheep
happy
chewing cauliflower with various good friends
in a sloping field
            when an old farmer in gumboots
his cap worn backwards, unlatches the
top gate with a bustling black-and-white
dog – and we
            bleat complaints about this
and, pretending we are doing it for
reasons of our own, we huddle into a
small, slow, shamefaced group
            and trot away
back where we should have been.

ALAN BROWNJOHN

The Sheep

Lazy sheep, pray tell me why
In the pleasant fields you lie,
Eating grass and daisies white,
From the morning till the night?
Everything can something do,
But what kind of use are you?

'Nay, my little master, nay,
Do not serve me so, I pray;
Don't you see the wool that grows
On my back to make you clothes?
Cold, and very cold, you'd be
If you had not wool from me.

True, it seems a pleasant thing
To nip the daisies in the spring;
But many chilly nights I pass
On the cold and dewy grass,
Or pick a scanty dinner, where
All the common's brown and bare.

Then the farmer comes at last,
When the merry spring is past,
And cuts my woolly coat away,
To warm you in the winter's day:
Little master, this is why
In the pleasant fields I lie.'

ANN and JANE TAYLOR

Sheep

The mothers have come back
From the shearing, and behind the hedge
The woe of sheep is like a battlefield
In the evening, when the fighting is over,
And the cold begins, and the dew falls,
And bowed women move with water.
Mother Mother Mother the lambs
Are crying, and the mothers are crying.
Nothing can resist that probe, that cry
Of a lamb for its mother, or a ewe's crying
For its lamb. The lambs cannot find
Their mothers among those shorn strangers.
A half-hour they have lamented,
Shaking their voices in desperation.
Bald brutal-voiced mothers braying out,
Flat-tongued lambs chopping off hopelessness
Their hearts are in panic, their bodies
Are a mess of woe, woe they cry,
They mingle their trouble, a music
Of worse and worse distress, a worse entangling,
They hurry out little notes
With all their strength, cries searching this way and that.
The mothers force out sudden despair, blaaa!
On restless feet, with wild heads.

Their anguish goes on and on, in the June heat.
Only slowly their hurt dies, cry by cry,
As they fit themselves to what has happened.

TED HUGHES

The New Pullets

Strangers inside their netted run,
They beak and pry;
They move with soft and clucking call –
Some brown, some burnished red, and all
Superbly shy.

Behind them stands their wooden house
That smells of tar;
And look – already through the door
One bird creeps in to where the four
Nest-boxes are.

There in the dark, remembering
The ancient law,
She does what law and nature bid,
And settles rustlingly amid
Her gathered straw.

Let us peep in. Ah, now she stands
On thoughtful leg
Into the nest-box peering down!
And on the straw – round, warm and brown –
See, her first egg!

JOHN WALSH

Maud's Children

Maud, in her long feathered trousers,
broods lovingly over her bantam chicks,
counting them aloud (rather tiresomely) all day,
one, two, three, four, five AND, believe it or not, six!

Their small brown velveteen bodies
bounce about in aimless animation;
they hop up and down, and scream things to each other
in high pitched voices trembling with indignation.

To judge from their state of turmoil,
all are presumably catching last trains,
as breathlessly, still shouting instructions, they race
tripping over things, into the darkness of drains,

only to reappear half crazed
by the ghastly things they have nearly seen,
to gallop with smothering sobs into the soon-
discovered ghastliness of the threshing machine.

With great difficulty they climb
on to Maud's back, stagger groggily around,
peer vertiginously over her wings and then
closing their eyes fall with a shrill shriek to the ground.

They spin and slip up and slither
like a crowd of hysterical skaters,
and though I know they are dear Maud's children they look
like mentally deficient bumblebees in gaiters.

VIRGINIA GRAHAM

Foul Fowl

Mum says, 'Hens are fowl,'
I think they're a bit strange, but not quite that bad.
They stop in mid-step
with one leg stuck up in the air
as though they've forgotten how to walk.
When they want to look at you
they have to turn their heads so much to one side
I think they must have very poor eyesight;
my dad squints when he can't find his glasses
but even he doesn't have to turn his head completely
to one side when he wants to see something.
I feel sorry for hens,
apart from having poor eyesight
it must be difficult walking on your back legs
all the time.
I wonder what happened to their front legs?

FRANK FLYNN

Song of the Battery Hen

We can't grumble about accommodation:
we have a new concrete floor that's
always dry, four walls that are
painted white, and a sheet-iron roof
the rain drums on. A fan blows warm air
beneath our feet to disperse the smell
of chicken-shit and, on dull days,
fluorescent lighting sees us.

You can tell me: if you come by
the North door, I am in the twelfth pen
on the left-hand side of the third row
from the floor; and in that pen
I am usually the middle one of three.
But, even without directions, you'd
discover me. I have the same orange-
red comb, yellow beak and auburn
feathers, but as the door opens and you
hear above the electric fan a kind of
one-word wail, I am the one
who sounds loudest in my head.

Listen. Outside this house there's an
orchard with small moss-green apple
trees; beyond that, two fields of
cabbages; then, on the far side of
the road, a broiler house. Listen:
one cockerel grows out of there, as
tall and proud as the first hour of sun.
Sometimes I stop calling with the others
to listen, and wonder if he hears me.

The next time you come here, look for me.
Notice the way I sound inside my head.
God made us all quite differently,
and blessed us with this expensive home.

EDWIN BROCK

Trouvée

(for Mr Wheaton Galentine and Mr Harold Leeds)

Oh, why should a HEN
have been run over
on West 4th Street
in the middle of summer?

She was a white hen
– red and white now, of course.
How did she get there?
Where was she going?

Her wing feathers spread
flat, flat in the tar,
all dirtied and thin
as tissue paper.

A pigeon, yes,
or an English sparrow,
might meet such a fate,
but not that poor fowl.

Just now I went back
to look again,
I hadn't dreamed it:
there is a hen

turned into a quaint
old country saying
scribbled in chalk
(except for the beak).

ELIZABETH BISHOP

Dobbin

The old horse, Dobbin,
  Out at grass
Turns his tail
  To the winds that pass;

And stares at the white road
  Winding down
Through the dwindling fields
  To the distant town.

He hears in the distance,
  A snip-snap trot,
He sees his master,
  A small dark dot,

Riding away
  On the smart new mare
That came last month
  From Pulborough Fair.

Dobbin remembers,
  As horses may,
How often he trotted
  That ringing way.

His coat is ragged
   And blown awry.
He droops his head
   And he knows not why.

Something has happened.
   Something has gone,
The world is changing,
   His work is done.

But his old heart aches
   With a heavier load
As he stands and wonders
   And stares at the road.

ALFRED NOYES

Old Horse

He's worked out
like a lead-mine, grey
dusty deserted,
lost for metal hammering metal,
clatter of feet and gear.

Head hung over a gate,
lower lip drooped
disconsolate,
he stands unmoving.
Then suddenly flings his mane
whipping a gauze of flies
that suck the juices
round suppurating eyes.

71

No one comes
to lead him to the stable, feed him oats
and polish his flanks to silver,
Lead-grey, weight
carried on three legs,
he sags with the sodden day
wrong side of the gate.

PHOEBE HESKETH

Nicholas Nye

Thistle and darnel and dock grew there,
  And a bush, in the corner, of may,
On the orchard wall I used to sprawl
  In the blazing heat of the day;
Half asleep and half awake,
  While the birds went twittering by,
And nobody there my lone to share
  But Nicholas Nye.

Nicholas Nye was lean and grey,
  Lame of a leg and old,
More than a score of donkey's years
  He had seen since he was foaled;
He munched the thistles, purple and spiked,
  Would sometimes stoop and sigh,
And turn his head, as if he said,
  'Poor Nicholas Nye!'

Alone with his shadow he'd drowse in the meadow,
  Lazily swinging his tail,
At break of day he used to bray, –
  Not much too hearty and hale;
But a wonderful gumption was under his skin,
  And a clear calm light in his eye,
And once in a while: he'd smile . . .
  Would Nicholas Nye.

Seem to be smiling at me, he would,
  From his bush, in the corner, of may, –
Bony and ownerless, widowed and worn,
  Knobble-kneed, lonely and grey;
And over the grass would seem to pass
  'Neath the deep dark blue of the sky,
Something much better than words between me
  And Nicholas Nye.

But dusk would come in the apple boughs,
  The green of the glow-worm shine,
The birds in nest would crouch to rest,
  And home I'd trudge to mine;
And there, in the moonlight, dark with dew,
  Asking not wherefore nor why,
Would brood like a ghost, and as still as a post,
  Old Nicholas Nye.

WALTER DE LA MARE

The Ass

Poor patient creature how I grieve to see
Thy wants so ill supplied – to see thee strain
and stretch thy tether for the grass in vain
Which heavens rain waters for all else but thee
The fair green field the fullness of the plain
Add to thy hunger colt and heifer pass
and roll as though they mocked thee on the grass
Which would be luxury to the bare brown lane
Where thou'rt imprisoned humble patient ass
Cropping foul weeds and scorning to complain.
Mercy at first 'sent out the wild ass free'
A ranger 'of the mountains' and what crimes
Did thy progenitors that thou shouldst be
The slave and mockery of latter times.

JOHN CLARE

The Duck

Behold the duck.
It does not cluck.
A cluck it lacks.
It quacks.
It is especially fond
Of a puddle or a pond.
When it dines or sups,
It bottoms ups.

OGDEN NASH

Quack!

The duck is whiter than whey is,
His tail tips up over his back,
The eye in his head is as round as a button,
And he says, QUACK! QUACK!

He swims on his bright blue mill pond,
By the willow tree under the shack,
Then stands on his head to see down to the bottom,
And says, QUACK! QUACK!

When Mollie steps out of the kitchen,
For apron – pinned round with a sack;
He squints at her round face, her dish, and what's in it,
And says, QUACK! QUACK!

He preens the pure snow of his feathers
In the sun by the wheat-straw stack;
At dusk waddles home with his brothers and sisters,
And says, QUACK! QUACK!

WALTER DE LA MARE

A True-blue Gentleman

This gentleman the charming duck
Quack quack says he
My tail's on
Fire, but he's only kidding

You can tell that

By his grin
He's one big grin, from wobbly
Feet to wobbly tail
Quack quack he tells us

Tail's on fire again

Ah yes
This charming gentleman the duck
With
His quaint alarms and
Trick of walking like a
Drunken hat
Quack quack says he

There's your fried egg

KENNETH PATCHEN

Duck

She waddles through the dust
In which no fish are smiling
Within her sides she carries
The restlessness of water

Clumsy
She waddles slowly
The reeds she's thinking of
She'll reach them anyway

Never
Never will she be able
To walk
As she was able
To plough the mirrors.

VASKO POPA
(translated by A. Pennington)

Ducks

1.

From troubles of the world
I turn to ducks,
Beautiful comical things
Sleeping or curled
Their heads beneath white wings
By water cool,
Or finding curious things
To eat in various mucks
Beneath the pool,
Tails uppermost, or waddling
Sailor-like on the shores
Of ponds, or paddling
– Left! right! – with fanlike feet
Which are for steady oars
When they (white galleys) float
Each bird a boat
Rippling at will the sweet
Wide waterway . . .
When night is fallen YOU creep
Upstairs, but drakes and dillies
Nest with pale water-stars,
Moonbeams and shadow bars,
And water-lilies:

Fearful too much to sleep
Since they've no locks
To click against the teeth
Of weasel and fox.
And warm beneath
Are eggs of cloudy green
Whence hungry rats and lean
Would stealthily suck
New life, but for the mien,
The bold ferocious mien
Of the mother-duck.

Yes, ducks are valiant things
On nests of twigs and straws,
And ducks are soothy things
And lovely on the lake
When that the sunlight draws
Thereon their pictures dim
In colours cool.
And when beneath the pool
They dabble, and when they swim
And make their rippling rings,
O ducks are beautiful things!

But ducks are comical things: –
As comical as you.
Quack!
They waddle round, they do.
They eat all sorts of things,
And then they quack.
By barn and stable and stack
They wander at their will,
But if you go too near
They look at you through black
Small topaz-tinted eyes
And wish you ill.
Triangular and clear
They leave their curious track
In mud at the water's edge,
And there amid the sedge
And slime they gobble and peer
Saying 'Quack! Quack!'

When God had finished the stars and whirl of coloured suns
He turned His mind from big things to fashion little ones.
Beautiful things (like daisies) He made, and then
He made the comical ones in case the minds of men

Should stiffen and become
  Dull, humourless and glum:
And so forgetful of their Maker be
As to take even themselves – QUITE SERIOUSLY.
Caterpillars and cats are lively and excellent puns:
All God's jokes are good – even the practical ones!
And as for the duck, I think God must have have smiled a bit
Seeing those bright eyes blink on the day He fashioned it.
And He's probably laughing still at the sound that came out of
its bill

F. W. HARVEY

The Poor Man's Pig

Already fallen plum-bloom stars the green
And apple-boughs as knarred as old toad's backs
Wear their small roses ere a rose is seen;
  The building thrush watches old Job who stacks
The bright-peeled osiers on the sunny fence,
  The pent sow grunts to hear him stumping by,
And tries to push the bolt and scamper thence,
  But her ringed snout still keeps her to the sty.

Then out he lets her run; away she snorts
  In bundling gallop for the cottage door,
With hungry hubbub begging crusts and orts,
  Then like a whirlwind bumping round once more;
Nuzzling the dog, making the pullets run,
  And sulky as a child when her play's done.

EDMUND BLUNDEN

The Prayer of the Little Pig

LORD,
their politeness makes me laugh!
Yes, I grunt!
Grunt and snuffle!
I grunt because I grunt
and snuffle
because I cannot do anything else!
All the same, I am not going to thank them
for fattening me up to make bacon.
Why did you make me so tender?
What a fate!
Lord,
teach me how to say
AMEN

CARMEN BERNOS DE GASZTOLD
(translated by Rumer Godden)

Bull Alone

Black bull, square and strong,
foursquare against the weather,
steams gently after rain—
bull-vapour spiralling gently into the hawthorn.
But he's young, ready to trample storms;
his meekness breaks under the hedge.
Stretching his neck he bellows the morning out,
trots to the gate barred
against acquiescent heifers,
roars over it his rage and grief,

rubs his sorrow along the top bar
then stands waiting
like an uncoupled engine, new but redundant.

Alone in a field wide for cavorting
among plentiful grass, unlaboured time,
he is sad as a caged lion,
energy dripping to waste,
triangular, rubbery tongue
mournfully licking his nostrils.

Away up in a gleam of blue
a lark is threading ascending beads of song
above five warm eggs in the grass.
The bull's ears turn, but his senses are raw
with angry suffering smelted in the blood
felt, not understood.

PHOEBE HESKETH

The Cow

The Cow is of the bovine ilk;
One end is moo, the other, milk.

OGDEN NASH

The Herd

How calmly cows move to the milking sheds,
How slowly, hieratically along,
How humbly with their moon-surmounted heads,
Though fly-pursued and stained, they pass me by
As gravely as the clouds across the sky,
They being, like the stars 'preserved from wrong'.

FRANCES CORNFORD

Milking Time

When supper time is almost come,
But not quite here, I cannot wait,
And so I take my china mug
And go down by the milking gate.
The cow is always eating shucks
And spilling off the little silk.
Her purple eyes are big and soft –
She always smells like milk.

And Father takes my mug from me,
And then he makes the stream come out.
I see it going in my mug
And foaming all about.

And when it's piling very high,
And when some little streams commence
To run and drip along the sides,
He hands it to me through the fence.

ELIZABETH MADOX ROBERTS

Cow in Meadow

All day
In a leisurely, kindly sort of way
She crops, and chews the grass,
And watches children as they pass
Through gentle, placid, wondering eyes.
Daylong, under quiet skies.
She crops and chews,
Uttering low and melancholy moos
For calves that came, and went again,
And left her lowing in the rain
How many weeks, months, years ago?
Thoughtful and slow
Her jaws work to and fro,
But like a flail
Her urgent, angry tail
Lashes at flies
That settle persistently on flanks and eyes.
All day she munches grass,
And munches grass,
Till the flies go
And evening shadows grow
And young boy's distant cry
'Coo-oo!' joins the rook-noise in the sky.
Then with a lurch she turns her head
Towards the cool, dark milking shed.

CLIVE SANSOM

Milking Song

Brownie, Brownie, let down your milk,
White as swansdown and smooth as silk,
Fresh as dew and pure as snow:
For I know where the cowslips blow,
And you shall have a cowslip wreath
No sweeter scented than your breath.

CHRISTINA ROSSETTI

Devon Cattle

They lug their churning bellies
like soft magnanimous factories.
Their cream fattens our strawberry guilt.

Flies cluster to drink their eyes.
Their calves are plundered on the night of birth.
The slow juices of their four guts
chink prompt on every doorstep in the land.

Now, suddenly, they have stopped us in this lane.
Swaying their heads, swaying their green-slimed haunches,
they moan and maunder, like the faithful in a procession
in some country we do not know. Timeless, engrossed,
they clog a highway, clinking little bells,
oblivious to all gods but the god of cows.

BRIAN JONES

Cow Pâté

The cow pat landed,
Settling in outflowing rings,
Rich, steaming, smelling of her.
She turns and tongues a mouth of grass,
Then follows
the pats
on
down
the
lane.

RONA M. CAMPBELL

AND THE SONG
OF A BIRD

Birds

A bird flies and has wings
And it certainly sings

A bird when it sings is always certain.
It sings and sings about certain things,
Like flying and having wings
Or being only a bird in a tree
And free

Free is when you are being certain
And wanting to sing certainly
About certain things.

A bird is free and certainly sings.
It sings and sings about flying and having wings
Or being always a certain thing
When it is only a bird in a tree
Singing certainly
And free.

RAY FABRIZIO

The Bird

As I went singing over the earth,
    Many a song I heard, –
A song of death and a song of mirth,
A song that was of little worth,
    And the song of a bird.

MARY COLERIDGE

Magpies

I have an orchard near my house,
　　Where poppies spread and corn has grown;
It is a holy place for weeds,
　　Where seeds stay on, and flower, till blown.
Into this orchard, wild and quiet,
　　The Magpie comes, the Owl and Rook:
To see one Magpie is not well,
　　But seeing two brings all good luck.
If Magpies think the same, and say,
　　'Two humans bring good luck, not one' –
How they must cheer us, Love, together,
　　And tremble when I come alone!

W. H. DAVIES

A Shot Magpie

Though on your long-tailed flight
You wore half-mourning of staid black and white,
So little did the thought of death
Enter the thievish head,
You never knew what choked your breath
When in a day turned night
You fell with feathers heavier than lead.

ANDREW YOUNG

Crows

I like to walk,
And hear the black crows talk.

I like to lie
And watch crows sail the sky.

I like the crow
That wants the wind to blow:

I like the one
That thinks the wind is fun.

I like to see
Crows spilling from a tree,

And try to find
The top crow left behind.

I like to hear
Crows caw that spring is near.

I like the great
Wild clamour of crow hate

Three farms away
When owls are out by day.

I like the slow
Tired home-ward flying crow;

I like the sight
Of crows for my good-night.

DAVID MCCORD

The Rooks

The rooks are building on the trees;
   They build there every spring:
'Caw, caw,' is all they say,
   For none of them can sing.

They're up before the break of day,
   And up till late at night;
For they must labour busily
   As long as it is light.

And many a crooked stick they bring,
   And many a slender twig,
And many a tuft of moss, until
   Their nests are round and big.

'Caw, caw.' Oh, what a noise
   They make in rainy weather!
Good children always speak by turns,
   But rooks all talk together.

AUNT EFFIE
(Jane Euphemia Browne)

The Cuckoo

The cuckoo and the warty toad
Digest the woolly caterpillar:

Only their toughened stomachs
Can cope with those poisonous hairs.

The cuckoo is footloose, irresponsible –
He scorns domestic cares,

And parks his ugly offspring on
His dupes, dunnock and titlark.

He's free to sing all day
His two-note song to his grey light-of-love;

And she replies, bubbling
Like water from a wide-necked bottle.

The cuckoo is a graceless, greedy bird –
And yet we love him still:

He told us spring had come. And all our days
We will remember cuckoo-time.

JOHN HEATH-STUBBS

The Eagle

He hangs between his wings outspread
    Level and still
And bends a narrow golden head,
    Scanning the ground to kill.

Yet as he sails and smoothly swings
    Round the hillside,
He looks as though from his own wings
    He hangs down crucified.

ANDREW YOUNG

The Eagle

He clasps the crag with crooked hands:
Close to the sun in lonely lands,
Ringed with the azure world, he stands.

The wrinkled sea beneath him crawls;
He watches from his mountain walls,
And like a thunderbolt he falls.

ALFRED LORD TENNYSON

The Feathers

(For Michaela)

On our early morning walk
learning about each other,
my three-year-old and I

discover a dead bird;
her first, so she must know
when it will wake and fly.

Now, it can't; the feathers are dead,
but the bird's in God's care.
Did He dead the feathers? leave them to dry

off that blood in the sun?
Wouldn't this one like to have breakfast?
Go back up in the sky

with all the other sparrows
Where is God's care? Will we
fall on the ground, die?

There's no construing the hieroglyphs of Death,
It has no grammar for the living.
Faced with it though, one has to try.

I tell what I hope is true,
making it simple. She's not alarmed,
head nodding acceptance. Yet her cry

bleeds across the blank of wind
like the call of some small bird:
But why Papa? Why? Papa why?

A. L. HENDRIKS

K is for Kestrel

Still hangs the Kestrel there
High in the still air
When the sky is fair.

So still he seems to stay
He might in the fair day
Be fixed there far away.

But presently he will
Swoop from his airy hill
And make some small bird still.

ELEANOR FARJEON

Sparrow

He's no artist.
His taste in clothes is more
dowdy than gaudy.
And his nest – that blackbird, writing
pretty scrolls on the air with the gold nib of his beak,
would call it a slum.

To stalk solitary on lawns,
to sing solitary in midnight trees,
to glide solitary over grey Atlantics –
not for him: he'd rather
a punch-up in a gutter.

He carries what learning he has
lightly – it is, in fact, based only
on the usefulness whose result
is survival. A proletarian bird.
No scholar.

But when winter soft-shoes in
and these other birds –
ballet dancers, musicians, architects –
die in the snow
and freeze to branches,
watch him happily flying
on the O-levels and A-levels
of the air.

NORMAN MACCAIG

Little Trotty Wagtail

Little trotty wagtail, he went in the rain,
And tittering tottering sideways, he near got straight again,
He stooped to get a worm, and look'd up to catch a fly,
And then he flew away ere his feathers they were dry.

Little trotty wagtail, he waddled in the mud,
And left his little footmarks, trample where he would.
He waddled in the water-pudge, and waggle went his tail,
And chirrup up his wings to dry upon the garden rail.

Little trotty wagtail, you nimble all about,
And in the dimpling water-pudge you waddle in and out,
Your home is nigh at hand, and in the warm pigsty,
So, little Master Wagtail, I'll bid you a good-bye.

JOHN CLARE

I Watched a Blackbird

I watched a blackbird on a budding sycamore
One Easter Day, when sap was stirring twigs to the core;
  I saw his tongue and crocus-coloured bill
  Parting and closing as he turned his trill;
  Then he flew down, seized on a stem of hay,
And upped to where his building scheme was underway,
As if so sure a nest were never shaped on spray.

THOMAS HARDY

The Blackbirds

There was an old man, in reproof
Of the blackbirds hob-nob in his cherries,
Cried: 'Be off now, you rascals, be off!'
But the rogues never stirred from the berries.
  They knew that his wits
  Were a little astray;
  They knew an old fogey it's
  Easy to prey,
So they merely sang sweeter to drown his reproof,
And the louder he called at them, 'Rascals, be off!'
  The merrier they in his cherries.

WALTER DE LA MARE

The Blackbird

'Sooty-plumed blackbird with your golden bill,
Why is your song so sweet and clear and mellow?'
'I lubricate my voice with slugs and snails.'
'And sometimes cherries, too?' 'Well, do you grudge me those –
Who pay you richly with a summer tune?'

JOHN HEATH-STUBBS

Dead Blackbird

The blackbird used to come each day
listening, head-sideways, for movement under the lawn,
stabbing his yellow-as-crocus bill
precisely in,
pulling out a pink elastic worm.

In winter with flirted tail
he landed on the sill for crumbs
ousting sparrows, blue-tits – even robins.
Soot-black, sleek,
his plumage shone like a dark man's head.

But this morning I looked out of the window
and saw him dead –
a crumpled bunch of feathers
rocking in the wind.

I have never seen anything dead
except flies
and stuffed animals in museums
where they make them look alive.

Dead people are hidden away,
tidied into boxes,
covered with flowers.
The living talk about the dead in low voices.
Is death so ugly, uncomfortable
that people are afraid?

I am much more afraid of what I cannot see.
But I can see the blackbird;
and I know these crumpled feathers
are only rags of him, not he
with his crocus-yellow bill.

PHOEBE HESKETH

Pigeons

Pigeons perch on the Holy Family
Carved over the west door on Joseph's head

On Mary's hand, making them smirk like humans
Who are kind to animals. Inside

The church now, we look out: the birds
Fly through the brown and scarlet saints, and crawl

Like sleepy wasps against their sandalled feet,
Lords of the window, devils looking in.

Then from the street a backfire sends them packing,
Only the stolid and the deaf stay on –

The saints are left to bow. The pigeons' wings
Clap round the square like faraway applause.

PATRICIA BEER

Swan

Swan, unbelievable bird, a cloud floating,
Arrangement of enormous white chrysanthemums
In a shop kept by angels, feathery statue
Carved from the fall of snow,

You are not too proud to take the crusts I offer.
You are so white that clear water stains you,
And I am ashamed that you have to swim
Here, where cigarette cartons hang in the lake,

And the plastic containers that held our ice-cream.
Now you bend your neck strong as a hawser
And I see your paddles like black rubber
Open and close as you move the webs of your swimming.

About you the small ducks, the coots, and the timid
Water-rails keep their admiring distances. Do not hurry.
Take what you need of my thrown bread, white swan,
Before you drift away, a cloud floating.

LESLIE NORRIS

Cock Pheasant

Halfway to school a pheasant flew overhead.
We all looked up, and then somebody said,
'O, if only I had a gun to shoot him dead.'
The very thought of it filled me with dread.
Fancy bringing down a lovely bird like that with lead,
With such splendid feathers of gold and red,
When all I wanted was to go on seeing him tread

Proudly in the wild woods where he was bred;
I could not bear to think of that bird lying on grassy bed,
Eyes empty of light, colours all shed.

LEONARD CLARK

Arithmetic

Those twittering swallows, hawking between the ricks –
The oddest theirs of all arithmetics!

Daring the seas, the cliffs of England won,
Two in late April came . . . Their housework done,
They conned this simple problem: – (1×1).

And lo! – in the evening sunshine, gilding the ricks –
Four fork-tailed fledglings, and the answer – six!

WALTER DE LA MARE

Heaven

The swallow with a chunk
of chalk in his beak
is going to scrawl across the sky:

'I am an aeroplane.
And if you don't believe me,
come up here and check.'

MICHELINE WANDOR

On Shooting a Swallow in Early Youth

I hoard a little spring of secret tears,
For thee, poor bird; thy death-blow was my crime;
From the far past it has flow'd on for years;
It never dries; it brims at swallow-time.
No kindly voice within me took thy part,
Till I stood o'er thy last faint flutterings;
Since then, methinks, I have a gentler heart,
And gaze with pity on all wounded wings.
Full oft the vision of thy fallen head,
Twitterings in highway dust, appeals to me;
Thy helpless form, as when I struck thee dead,
Drops out from every swallow-flight I see.
I would not have thine airy spirit laid,
I seem to love the little ghost I made.

CHARLES TENNYSON TURNER

The Linnet

Upon this leafy bush
   With thorns and roses in it,
Flutters a thing of light,
   A twittering linnet,
And all the throbbing world
   Of dew and sun and air
By this small parcel of life
   Is made more fair:
As if each bramble-spray
   And mounded gold-wreathed furze,

Harebell and little thyme,
  Were only hers;
As if this beauty and grace
  Did to one bird belong,
And, at a flutter of wing,
  Might vanish in song.

WALTER DE LA MARE

The Burial of the Linnet

Found in the garden – dead in his beauty.
  Ah, that a linnet should die in the spring!
Bury him, comrades, in pitiful duty,
  Muffle the dinner bell, solemnly ring.

Bury him kindly – up in the corner;
  Bird, beast, and goldfish are sepulchred there.
Bid the black kitten march as chief mourner,
  Waving her tale like a plume in the air.

Bury him nobly – next to the donkey;
  Fetch the old banner, and wave it about.
Bury him deeply – think of the monkey,
  Shallow his grave, and the dogs got him out.

Bury him softly – white wool around him,
  Kiss his poor feathers – the first kiss and last;
Tell his poor widow kind friends have found him:
  Plant his poor grave with whatever grows fast.

Farewell, sweet singer! dead in thy beauty,
　　Silent through summer, though other birds sing.
Bury him, comrades, in pitiful duty,
　　Muffle the dinner bell, mournfully ring.

JULIANA HORATIA EWING

The Righteous Mother

'Wretch!' cried the mother to her infant son.
'You hateful little boy, what have you done?
Killed the white butterfly, of all dear things,
And then pulled off his tiny, fairy wings.
To butterflies this garden is their home –
Here do they dance and kiss the flowers and roam
In happiness and plenty, even as you.
God would be very angry if He knew!'

And while she spoke these salutary words
Her hat displayed two withered humming-birds.

EDEN PHILPOTTS

Robin's Round

I am the proper
Bird for this season –
Not blessed St Turkey,
Born to be eaten.

I'm man's inedible
Permanent bird.
I dine in his garden,
My spoon is his spade.

I'm the true token
Of Christ the Child-King:
I nest in man's stable,
I eat at man's table,
Through all his dark winters
I sing.

U. A. FANTHORPE

Robin

With a bonfire throat,
Legs of twig,
A dark brown coat,
The inspector robin
Comes where I dig.

GELDART

Military man
With a bright eye
And a wooden leg,
He must scrounge and beg
Now the summer's by:

Beg at the doors,
Scrounge in the gardens,
While daylight lessens
And the grass glistens
And the ground hardens.

The toads have their vaults,
The squirrels their money,
The swifts their journey:
For him the earth's anger,
The taste of hunger.

And his unfrightened song
For the impending snows
Is also for the rose,
And for the great armada
And the Phoenician trader,
And the last missile raider –
It's the only one he knows.

HAL SUMMERS

THIS I REMEMBER

Squirrel up a Pole

The engine roar in lower gear
Bent up the squirrel in an arc of fear;
Black beads of panic twisted in his head
And in the switchboard of his agile brain
All lines were crossed.

Sense of direction lost
He darted through a tube of broken drain,
Anywhere to be free,
And threw himself against the nearest tree . . .
And panic made it any nearby tree,
One that was tall and straight and bare,
A columned, branchless path to anywhere.

Somehow his claws obeyed
And on the cross-piece at the top
He found the track
He'd chosen was a cul-de-sac.
Exposed, alone,
He feared the humming telephone
And leapt
Belly revealed and legs outswept,
Unorganized and splayed out tight
Into a clumsy tree-fox flight;
Denied an ordinary tree
He fell with little dignity,
Crashed, rolled, bounced up, was tossed,
Then scampering low-tailed
Got lost.

GREGORY HARRISON

117

The Fawn in the Snow

The brown-dappled fawn
Bereft of the doe
Shivers in blue shadow
Of the glaring snow,

His whole world bright
As a jewel, and hard,
Diamond white,
Turquoise barred.

The trees are black,
Their needles gold,
Their boughs crack
In the keen cold.

The brown-dappled fawn
Bereft of the doe
Trembles and shudders
At the bright snow.

The air whets
The warm throat,
The frost frets
At the smooth coat.

Brown agate eyes
Opened round
Agonize
At the cold ground,

At the cold heaven
Enamelled pale,
At the earth shriven
By the snowy gale,

At magic glitter
Burning to blind,
At beauty bitter
As an almond rind.

Fawn, fawn,
Seek for your south,
For kind dawn
With her cool mouth,

For green sod
With gold and blue
Dappled, as God
Has dappled you, . . .

The shivering fawn
Paws at the snow.
South and dawn
Lie below;

Richness and mirth,
Dearth forgiven,
A happy earth,
A warm heaven.

The sleet streams;
The snow flies;
The fawn dreams
With wide brown eyes.

WILLIAM ROSE BENÉT

In Midwinter a Wood was . . .

In midwinter a wood was
where the sand-coloured deer ran
through quietness.
It was a marvellous thing
to see those deer running.

Softer than ashes
snow lay all winter where they ran,
and in the wood a holly tree was.
God, it was a marvellous thing
to see the deer running.

Between lime trunks grey or green
branch-headed stags went by
silently trotting.
A holly tree dark and crimson
sprouted at the wood's centre, thick and high
without a whisper, no other berry so fine.

Outside the wood was black midwinter,
over the downs that reared so solemn
wind rushed in gales, and strong here
wrapped around wood and holly fire
(where deer among the close limes ran)
with a storming circle of its thunder.
Under the trees it was a marvellous thing
to see the deer running.

PETER LEVI

Deer

Such gentle things they are,
Stepping discreetly over the cropped turf;
Or moving noiselessly through woods,
Their smooth flanks flecked with sunlight.
Their eyes are calm as forest pools,
Unguarded, calm, reflective:
The world is watched through sensitive nostrils.
And when the wind (unfelt by us)
Warns them of danger, suddenly they are gone.
The woods are empty. The barred sunlight
Strikes across trunks only and stippled leaves.

CLIVE SANSOM

The Weasel

It should have been a moment
Of high drama,
The lithe, cigar-slim body,
The slight withdrawal and swift spring,
The soft explosion of black feathers . . .
But when I glided to a halt
And leaned from the car window
The blackbird had lost the duel
Of dignity,
And was being dragged,
Claws drooping palely
Upthrust on straw legs,
By the tiny killer,
Rump high, teeth gum-deep in feathers
Just above the two
Baby finger-nail eyelids.

The click of the ignition key
Startled the weasel
And through the verge grass he disappeared,
While the incongruous corpse
Stiffened in the dust.

But patience.
This plump prize whose blood
Is still, but still warm,
Is being watched,
And three anxious minutes pass
Before the grass
Parts,
The triangular, fawn head appears,
Looks up and down the lane,
Ignores the car,
And leaps to the carcass,

Drags it up the small cliff of the bank
And slides through the hedge backwards –
The whole action so neat,
Cool and efficient,
The work of a professional.

GREGORY HARRISON

Interruption to a Journey

The hare we had run over
Bounced about the road
On the springing curve
Of its spine.

Cornfields breathed in the darkness,
We were going through the darkness and
The breathing cornfields from one
Important place to another.

We broke the hare's neck
And made that place, for a moment,
The most important place there was,
Where a bowstring was cut
And a bow broken forever
That had shot itself through so many
Darknesses and cornfields.

It was left in that landscape.
It left us in another.

NORMAN MACCAIG

Who They Are

Wife and husband,
brother and sister,
neighbour and neighbour,
they lie there on the road.
I do not know
who they are
except that they
are dead,
not a whisker twitching.
The cars whiz by not noticing them.
But I do.
Further on in the road lies
a bundle
and another bundle.
I do not know
who they are
except that they
are dead,
not a feather stirring.
They used to be able
to run
and fly
across green safe fields.
But now there is a road.
Man has built a motorway.

CHARLOTTE HARVEY

Hare

There's something eerie about a hare, no matter how stringy
and old.
I heard of a hare caught in a snowdrift, brought in under a coat
from the cold
Turned by firelight into a tall fine woman who many a strange
tale told.

The hare has a powerful whiff with her, even when she's a pet,
Her back as broad and strong as a dog, and her kick like a bull-
calf, yet
Into your dreams she waltzes, strung with starlight and music, a
marionette.

They say it's a nude witch dancing her rings though it looks like
a lolloping hare
Circling the farm, like a full moon circling the globe, and
leaning to stare
Bulge-eyed in at the midnight window down at the sleeping
children there.

Something scares me about a hare, like seeing an escapee
From a looney-bin, lurching and loping along in his flapping
pyjamas, free –
Or meeting a woman mad with religion who has fastened her
eyes on me.

You'll never hurt a hare after you've heard her cry in pain.
A mother's scream, a baby's scream, and a needle slips in
through your ear and brain,
To prick and prick your heart when you hear of the hurt of a
hare again.

TED HUGHES

Hare

He lives on edge throughout his days,
home-fixated, short of sight,
dark heart beating as to burst his breast,
given to sudden panic fright
that sends him hurtling unpredictably
through crops, round quarries, over stones.
And has great eyes, all veined with blood,
and beautifully-articulated bones.

Superstition gives him an unchancy name,
any power that you might mention;
certainly he haunts the corner of the eye,
the edge of the attention
on open downs where movement is surprising,
caught and gone again with every glance,
or jack-knifing quietly through adjacent hedges
beyond the golden stubble-fires' dance.

But he is no more than flesh and blood,
living all his speedy life with fear,
only oblivious of constant danger
at his balletic time of year
when spring skies, winds, the greening furrows
overcome hunger, nervousness, poor sight,
fill him with urgent, huge heroics,
make him stand up and fight.

MOLLY HOLDEN

Rabbits

Rabbits have fur
And also more rabbits
And it is a habit.

A habit is something you are doing
Over and over again
Because you are liking it
When you have it.

A habit of rabbits is having more.
First there is a rabbit with fur
and you have it.
But soon there are more.

Soon they are having more rabbits
Over and over again and liking to do it
And then it is a habit
And rabbits really have it.

RAY FABRIZIO

Lonely Horse

Going to Birmingham by train I saw
A horse; not grazing but his head held low.
He stood unmoving and his brown-white nose
Was rounded. In the field stood nothing else –

Except the thistle islands in the cropped
Turf; though his vision of our land was stopped
By bordering hedges. I shall think of him
Still there when I've come back from Birmingham –

Especially when I'm sitting on the lawn,
Enclosed by garden walls. If any one
Looked over them he'd see my brown and white
Moustache and head bent downwards as I write.

ROY FULLER

The Pale Horse

I stared at the pale horse,
He stared back at me,
I did not know what he was thinking
Under his sunless tree,
But never before had I seen a horse
So sad and pale as he,
And did I seem to him
As black as ebony,
And the place where I was standing
As cold and shadowy?

LEONARD CLARK

A Memory

This I remember,
I saw from a train
A shaggy wild pony
That stood in the rain.

Where I was going,
And where was the train,
I cannot remember,
I cannot explain.

All these years after
It comes back again:
A shaggy wild pony
That stood in the rain.

DOUGLAS GIBSON

Horse

The picnickers were sleeping when I,
deciding to be an enormous black horse not seen
in the corner of their field, strolled over.

They had a tartan rug, and a
thermos flask, and they had unwrapped
and eaten little triangles of processed

cheese, with tomatoes. They had been
playing cards among the thistles and
water-biscuits, and had fallen asleep

in the very hot sun. So I was a sudden, black
alarming shadow standing over them, though really
just inquisitive. When one of them heard the sound of my
   breath,

and woke, having dreamt of dragons, and
leapt up and shouted, *I* had to pretend to
be frightened of *them* and gallop away.

ALAN BROWNJOHN

The Horse

The horse moves
independently
without reference
to his load.

He has eyes
like a woman and
turns them
about, throws

back his ears
and is generally
conscious of
the world. Yet

he pulls when
he must and
pulls well, blowing
fog from

his nostrils
like fumes from
the twin
exhausts of a car.

WILLIAM CARLOS WILLIAMS

At Grass

The eye can hardly pick them out
From the cold shade they shelter in,
Till wind distresses tail and mane;
Then one crops grass, and moves about
– The other seeming to look on –
And stands anonymous again.

Yet fifteen years ago, perhaps
Two dozen distances sufficed
To fable them: faint afternoons

Of Cups and Stakes and Handicaps,
Whereby their names were artificed
To inlay faded, classic Junes –

Silks at the start: against the sky
Numbers and parasols: outside,
Squadrons of empty cars, and heat,
And littered grass: then the long cry
Hanging unhushed till it subside
To stop-press columns on the street.

Do memories plague their ears like flies?
They shake their heads. Dusk brims the shadows.
Summer by summer all stole away,
The starting-gates, the crowds and cries –
All but the unmolesting meadows.
Almanacked, their names live; they

Have slipped their names, and stand at ease,
Or gallop for what must be joy,
And not a fieldglass sees them home,
Or curious stop-watch prophesies:
Only the groom, and the groom's boy,
With bridles in the evening come.

PHILIP LARKIN

There's a Toad in the Road at Piccadilly

There's a toad in the road at Piccadilly.
Eros is cross and looking silly.

O toad romantic
Corybantic
Flaunting in the neon glow
Jaunting on jurassic toe.

Toad florescent
Erubescent
Ululating by the gutter
Coruscating through the clutter.

Dancing toad
Entrancing toad
Crooning a reptilian sonnet
In your tam o'shanter bonnet.

Toad poetic
Toad balletic
Skimming through department stores
With a rose between your jaws,
Twinkling down the lighted street,
Toad your eyes are sad and sweet,
Toad my life is incomplete.

I, incessantly lamenting,
Watch your disappearing feet,
Weeping at this strange absenting.

Toad your heart is made of granite,
Your disdain is unrelenting,
Softly to a fading planet,
I alone intone an ode.

There's a toad in the road at Piccadilly
Eros is cross and looking silly.

JOHN WHITWORTH

Black Dot

a black dot
a jelly tot

a scum-nail
a jiggle-tail

a cool kicker
a sitting slicker

a panting puffer
a fly-snuffer

a high-hopper
a belly-flopper

a catalogue
to make me
FROG

LIBBY HOUSTON

Halfway

I saw a tadpole once in a sheet of ice
(a freakish joke played by my country's weather).
He hung at arrest, displayed as it were in glass,
an illustration of neither one thing nor the other.

His head was a frog's and his hinder legs had grown
ready to climb and jump to his promised land;
but his bladed tail in the ice-pane weighed him down.
He seemed to accost my eye with his budding hand.

'I am neither one thing nor the other, not here nor there.
I saw great lights in the place where I would be,
but rose too soon, half made for water, half air,
and they have gripped and stilled and enchanted me.

'Is that world real, or a dream I cannot reach?
Beneath me the dark familiar waters flow
and my fellows huddle and nuzzle each to each,
while motionless here I stare where I cannot go.'

The comic O of his mouth, his gold-rimmed eyes,
looked in that lustrous gaze as though they'd ask
my vague divinity, looming in stooped surprise,
for death or rescue. But neither was my task.

Waking halfway from a dream one winter night
I remembered him as a poem I had to write.

                                    JUDITH WRIGHT

Toad

Stop looking like a purse. How could a purse
squeeze under the rickety door and sit,
full of satisfaction, in a man's house?

You clamber towards me on your four corners –
one hand, one foot, one hand, one foot.

I love you for being a toad,
for crawling like a Japanese wrestler,
and for not being frightened.

I put you in my purse hand, not shutting it,
and set you down outside directly under
every star.

A jewel in your head? Toad,
you've put one in mine,
a tiny radiance in a dark place.

NORMAN MACCAIG

Frog and Toad

Hopping frog, hop here and be seen,
  I'll not pelt you with stick or stone:
Your cap is laced and your coat is green:
  Goodbye, we'll let each other alone.

Plodding toad, plod here and be looked at,
You the finger of scorn is crooked at:
But though you're lumpish, you're harmless too;
You won't hurt me, and I won't hurt you.

CHRISTINA ROSSETTI

A Friend in the Garden

He is not John the gardener,
  And yet the whole day long
Employs himself most usefully,
  The flower beds among.

He is not Tom the pussy cat,
  And yet the other day,
With stealthy stride and glistening eye,
  He crept upon his prey.

He is not Dash the dear old dog,
  And yet, perhaps, if you
Took pains with him and petted him,
  You'd come to love him too.

He's not a blackbird, though he chirps,
  And though he once was black;
And now he wears a loose grey coat,
  All wrinkled on the back.

He's got a very dirty face,
  And very shining eyes;
He sometimes comes and sits indoors;
  He looks – and p'r'aps is – wise.

But in a sunny flower bed
  He has a fixed abode;
He eats the things that eat my plants –
  He is a friendly TOAD.

JULIANA HORATIA EWING

Little Frog

Little frog among
rain-shaken leaves, are you, too,
splashed with green paint?

GAKI

The Frog

The Frog by Nature is both damp and cold,
Her Mouth is large, her Belly much will hold:
She sits somewhat ascending, loves to be
Croaking in Gardens, though unpleasantly. . . .

JOHN BUNYAN

Frogs

Frogs sit more solid
Than anything sits. In mid-leap they are
Parachutists falling
In a free fall. They die on roads
With arms across their chests and
Heads high.

I love frogs that sit
Like Buddha, that fall without
Parachutes, that die
Like Italian tenors.

Above all, I love them because
Pursued in water, they never
Panic so much that they fail
To make stylish triangles
With their ballet dancer's legs.

NORMAN MACCAIG

All I Intended to do was Pass

All I intended to do was pass
Yet he refused to budge, a hefty, angle-faced cross-breed,
His physique stupendous, the build of a St Bernard.
But his mind was puny.
A mammoth-sized dog, he could not sense that,
All I wanted to do was pass.
His round lovable eyes stared at me.
It was clear, he took me for a friend.
All I wanted to do was pass.
But he was there.
He seemed to beg for help.
His eyes widened, he sensed the opportunity and moved his
    paw.
Stroking it on my shoe.
All I wanted to do was pass.
I felt pity for him, one couldn't help it.
Scruffy, fluffy and senseless.
I couldn't help pitying him.
I was tempted to stroke him, but refrained.
He shuffled closer.
All I wanted to do was pass.
I did stroke him, he was sensitive to my stroking.
His eyes seemed to tell me he liked me
I couldn't help it, I returned his affections
I wanted him now – I needed him
No collar, no identification tag
I could have him – I could,
And yet all I wanted to do was pass.

BARRY WILLIAMS

Cat in Winter

Look now at that
soft-footed, elegant cat,
hard, amber eyes,
set on an enterprise,
playful or grim,
known only to him,
slinking through snow.
Watch him cunningly go
along his chosen track,
the one touch of black
in a world of white,
as if with second sight
he clearly knew
his rendezvous
where he will stay
the best part of the day,
hidden by heavy trees,
ready to pounce and seize
some bird that's unaware
danger is lurking there.
Will wait an hour to kill
his harmless prey, until
he hears the tell-tale cheep,
and makes his leap.
Satisfied, will then return
the way that earlier he came.
He feels no guilt or shame,
with minimum of fuss
strolls back to us,
does not pretend
snow is a bosom friend,
nor we his kith and kin,
and we shall let him in.

For all his character
hear him gently purr,
play with his paws,
forgetting he has claws.

LEONARD CLARK

Diamond Cut Diamond

Two cats
One up a tree
One under the tree
The cat up a tree is he
The cat under the tree is she
The tree is witch elm, just incidentally.
He takes no notice of she, she takes no notice of he.
He stares at the woolly clouds passing, she stares at the tree.
There's been a lot written about cats, by Old Possum, Yeats and Company
But not Alfred de Musset or Lord Tennyson or Poe or anybody
Wrote about one cat under, and one cat up, a tree.
God knows why this should be left for me
Except I like cats as cats be
Especially one cat up
And one under
A witch elm
Tree

EWART MILNE

Cat

Cat, nine days old, knit out of soot,
Fragile and scrawny, squirms in the cupped palm;
Mewls, pukes, and gestures with four needy paws:
Milk; sleep; warmth; that brusque abrasive tongue
Which scours, explores the rank damp-clinging fur
Already cat, not pussy
                            – yet he learns
To live that part: house-trained, and neatly vetted,
Sleeks out to plump domestic, cuddles up,
Rolling a musky jowl on chair or shoe;
Purr modulates, and claws retract,
Till puss in jackboots serves for pantomime
And housewife's matinée.
                            But that's his guile: to mince
With delicate correctness, bland as cream,
Among the best tea-service; lapped in silk,
Conceals a yawn (eyes wincing cosily)

To watch a stooge pull strings, feed him a line,
Or mime his mousing with a ball of wool
Juggled
        – until he strikes,
Spins it off axis, sinks five searing claws
Deep into Europe, and begins
Unravelling the globe.

WILLIAM DUNLOP

To a Young Cat in the Orchard

Elegant creature with black shoulders bent,
Stalking the bird in song,
To what intent?
Tell what a wild source brims those empty eyes,
What well of shameless light,
Beyond the bounds of Hell or Paradise
Or wrong
Or right.

FRANCES CORNFORD

The Rat

Strange that you let me come so near
    And send no questing senses out
From eye's dull jelly, shell-pink ear,
    Fierce-whiskered snout.

But clay has hardened in these claws
    And gypsy-like I read too late
In lines scored on your naked paws
    A starry fate.

Even that snake, your tail, hangs dead,
    And as I leave you stiff and still
A death-like quietness has spread
    Across the hill.

ANDREW YOUNG

The Fieldmouse

Where the acorn tumbles down,
   Where the ash tree sheds its berry,
With your fur so soft and brown,
   With your eye so round and merry,
Scarcely moving the long grass,
Fieldmouse, I can see you pass.

Little thing, in what dark den,
   Lie you all the winter sleeping?
Till warm weather comes again,
   Then once more I see you peeping
Round about the tall tree roots,
Nibbling at their fallen fruits.

Fieldmouse, fieldmouse, do not go,
   Where the farmer stacks his treasure,
Find the nut that falls below,
   Eat the acorn at your pleasure,
But you must not steal the grain
He has stacked with so much pain.

Make your hole where mosses spring,
   Underneath the tall oak's shadow,
Pretty, quiet, harmless thing,
   Play about the sunny meadow.
Keep away from corn and house,
None will harm you, little mouse.

CECIL FRANCES ALEXANDER

Harvest Mouse

A sleek, brown acrobat, he climbs
The golden cornstalk till it sways
And sags beneath him. As it swings,
His tail-end twines a neighbour stalk
And balancing with tail and claw
He climbs aloft until he finds
The crisp, ripe, bristly ear of corn;
Then lies along its tilting length,
As if all corn-ears were created
For mice to nibble at . . . and nibbles.

CLIVE SANSOM

Bah!

When I chanced to look over the wall in the glade –
I was taking a walk with Mamma –
I saw an old ewe sitting down in the shade,
    And she opened her mouth and said 'Bah!'

That's always what happens when sheep I come near,
They watch me approach from afar,
And out of the clover and turnips I hear
A horrid ironical 'Bah!'

What can I have done? I can't understand –
The cantankerous creatures they are!
I never throw stones, I hold dear Mamma's hand,
And I don't think they ought to say 'Bah!'

WALTER DE LA MARE

here's a little mouse

here's a little mouse) and
what does he think about, i
wonder as over this
floor (quietly with

bright eyes) drifts (nobody
can tell because
Nobody knows, or why
jerks Here &, here,
gr(oo)ving the room's Silence) this like
a littlest
poem a
(with wee ears and see?

tail frisks)
       (gonE)
'mouse',
      We are not the same you and
i, since here's a little he
or is
it It
? (or was something we saw in the mirror)?

therefore we'll kiss; for maybe
what was Disappeared
into ourselves
who (look).   , startled

                e. e. cummings

The Mole

Small piteous thing in the sun's yellow blaze
Cold, motionless – how came
Thy feet to lose those winding darkened ways –
Those lovable small roads beneath the sward
Where thou didst live, and play full many a game
With velvet-coated brethren? What reward
Lured thee to light
From thine own natural night?

Thou has no wound upon thee: yet art dead –
Stretched on that greenery
Which laid a summer thatching for thy head
In homely rooms of darkness under the ground.
And now the alien sunlight falls on thee;
Breeze ruffles thy soft coat: and all around
Bloom red and gold
Flowers thou didst ne'er behold.

Didst go a-wandering, and lose thy way,
Then suddenly warmth and wind
Encounter? Did the wonder of the day
Beat like a voice upon thy shuttered soul
To tell thee cruelly that thou wert blind,
And make thee know thyself a little mole
With pushing snout,
From worlds of light shut out?

F. W. HARVEY

The Ballad of Red Fox

Yellow sun yellow
Sun yellow sun,
When, oh, when
Will red fox run?

When the hollow horn shall sound,
When the hunter lifts his gun
And liberates the wicked hound,
Then, oh, then shall red fox run.

Yellow sun yellow
Sun yellow sun,
Where, oh, where
Will red fox run?

Through meadows hot as sulphur,
Through forests cool as clay,
Through hedges crisp as morning
And grasses limp as day.

Yellow sky yellow
Sky yellow sky,
How, oh, how
Will red fox die?

With a bullet in his belly,
A dagger in his eye,
And blood upon his red red brush
Shall red fox die.

MELVIN WALKER LA FOLLETTE

A Fellow Mortal

I found a fox, caught by the leg
In a toothed gin, torn from its peg,
And dragged, God knows how far, in pain.

Such torment could not plead in vain,
He looked at me, I looked at him,
With iron jaw-teeth in his limb.

'Come, little son,' I said, 'Let be . . .
Don't bite me, while I set you free.'

But much I feared that in the pang
Of helping, I should feel a fang
In hand or face . . .

                          but must is must . . .
And he had given me his trust.

So down I knelt there in the mud
And loosed those jaws all mud and blood.
And he, exhausted, crept, set free,
Into the shade, away from me;

The leg not broken . . .

                          Then, beyond,
That gin went plonk into the pond.

JOHN MASEFIELD

Small, Smaller

I thought that I knew all there was to know
Of being small, until I saw once, black against the snow,
A shrew, trapped in my footprint, jump and fall
And jump again and fall, the hole too deep, the walls too tall.

RUSSELL HOBAN

OF ALL THE
TREASURES THAT
WERE MINE

A Child's Dream

I had a little dog, and my dog was very small;
He licked me in the face, and he answered to my call;
Of all the treasures that were mine, I loved him most of all.

His nose was fresh as morning dew and blacker than the night;
I thought that it could even snuff the shadows and the light;
And his tail he held bravely, like a banner in a fight.

His body covered thick with hair was very good to smell;
His little stomach underneath was pink as any shell;
And I loved him and honoured him, more than words can tell.

We ran out in the morning, both of us, to play,
Up and down across the fields for all the sunny day;
But he ran so swiftly – he ran right away.

I looked for him, I called for him, entreatingly. Alas,
The dandelions could not speak, though they had seen him
     pass,
And nowhere was his waving tail among the waving grass.

I called him in a thousand ways and yet he did not come;
The pathways and the hedges were horrible and dumb.
I prayed to God who never heard. My desperate soul grew
     numb.

The sun sank low. I ran; I prayed: 'If God has not the power
To find him, let me die. I cannot bear another hour.'
When suddenly I came upon a great yellow flower.

And all among its petals, such was Heaven's grace,
In that golden hour, in that golden place,
All among its petals, was his hairy face.

FRANCES CORNFORD

Two Dogs Have I

For years we've had a little dog,
Last year we acquired a big dog;
He wasn't big when we got him,
He was littler than the dog we had.
We thought our little dog would love him,
Would help him to become a trig dog,
But the new little dog got bigger,
And the old little dog got mad.

Now the big dog loves the little dog,
But the little dog hates the big dog,
The little dog is eleven years old,
And the big dog only one;
The little dog calls him *Schweinhund*,
The little dog calls him Pig-dog,
She grumbles broken curses
As she dreams in the August sun.

The big dog's teeth are terrible,
But he wouldn't bite the little dog;
The little dog wants to grind his bones,
But the little dog has no teeth;
The big dog is acrobatic,
The little dog is a brittle dog;
She leaps to grip his jugular,
And passes underneath.

The big dog clings to the little dog
Like glue and cement and mortar;
The little dog is his own true love;
But the big dog is to her
Like a scarlet rag to a Longhorn,
Or a suitcase to a porter;
The day he sat on the hornet
I distinctly heard her purr.

Well, how can you blame the little dog,
Who was once the household darling?
He romps like a young Adonis,
She droops like an old moustache;
No wonder she steals his corner,
No wonder she comes out snarling,
No wonder she calls him *Cochon*
And even *Espèce de vache*.

Yet once I wanted a sandwich,
Either caviare or cucumber,
When the sun had not yet risen
And the moon had not yet sank;
As I tiptoed through the hallway
The big dog lay in slumber,
And the little dog slept by the big dog,
And her head was on his flank.

OGDEN NASH

The Caged Bird in Springtime

What can it be
This curious anxiety?
It is as if I wanted
To fly away from here.

But how absurd!
I have never flown in my life,
And I do not know
What flying means, though I have heard,
Of course, something about it.

Why do I peck the wires of this little cage?
It is the only nest I have ever known.
But I want to build my own,
High in the secret branches of the air.

I cannot quite remember how
It is done, but I know
That what I want to do
Cannot be done here.

I have all I need –
Seed and water, air and light.
Why, then, do I weep with anguish,
And beat my head and my wings
Against these sharp wires, while the children
Smile at each other, saying: 'Hark how he sings'?

JAMES KIRKUP

Dog

O little friend, your nose is ready; you sniff,
Asking for that expected walk,
(Your nostrils full of the happy rabbit-whiff)
And almost talk.

And so the moment becomes a moving force;
Coats glide down from their pegs in the humble dark;

You scamper the stairs,
Your body informed with the scent and the track and the mark
Of stoats and weasels, moles and badgers and hares.

We are going *Out*. You know the pitch of the word,
Probing the tone of thought as it comes through fog
And reaches by devious means (half-smelt, half-heard)
The four-legged brain of a walk-ecstatic dog.

Out through the garden your head is already low.
You are going your walk, you know,
And your limbs will draw
Joy from the earth through the touch of your padded paw.

Now, sending a little look to us behind,
Who follow slowly the track of your lovely play,
You fetch our bodies forward away from mind
Into the light and fun of your useless day.

Thus, for your walk, we took ourselves, and went
Out by the hedge, and tree, to the open ground.
You ran, in delightful strata of wafted scent,
Over the hill without seeing the view;
Beauty is hinted through primitive smells to you:
And that ultimate Beauty you track is but rarely found.

Home . . . and further joy will be waiting there:
Supper full of the lovely taste of bone.
You lift up your nose again, and sniff, and stare
For the rapture known

Of the quick wild gorge of food, then the still lie-down;
While your people will talk above you in the light
Of candles, and your dreams will merge and drown
Into the bed-delicious hours of night.

HAROLD MONRO

Our Hamster's Life

Our hamster's life:
there's not much
to it,
not much
to it.

He presses his pink nose
to the door of his cage
and decides for the fifty six
millionth time
that he can't get
through it.

Our hamster's life:
there's not much
to it,
not much
to it.

It's about the most boring
life in the world
if he only
knew it.
He sleeps and he drinks and he eats.
He eats and he drinks and he sleeps.

He slinks and he dreeps.
He eats.

This process
he repeats.

Our hamster's life:
there's not much
to it,
not much
to it.

You'd think it would drive him bonkers,
going round and round on his wheel.
It's certainly driving me bonkers,

watching him
do it.

But he may be thinking:
'That boy's life,
there's not much
to it,
not much
to it:

watching a hamster go round on a wheel,
It's driving me bonkers if he only knew it,

watching him
watching me
do it.'

KIT WRIGHT

D is for Dog

My dog went mad and bit my hand,
   I was bitten to the bone:
My wife went walking out with him,
   And then came back alone.

I smoked my pipe, I nursed my wound,
   I saw them both depart:
But when my wife came back alone,
   I was bitten to the heart.

W. H. DAVIES

O Pug!

*To the Brownes' pug dog,
on my lap, in their car,
coming home from Norfolk*

O Pug, some people do not like you
But I like you,
Some people say you do not breathe, you snore,
I don't mind,
One person says he is always conscious of your behind,
Is that your fault?

Your own people love you,
All the people in the family that owns you
Love you: Good pug, they cry, Happy pug,
Pug-come-for-a-walk.

You are an old dog now
And in all your life
You have never had cause for a moment's anxiety,
Yet,
In those great eyes of yours,
Those liquid and protuberant orbs,
Lies the shadow of immense insecurity. There
Panic walks.

Yes, yes, I know,
When your mistress is with you,
When your master
Takes you upon his lap,
Just then, for a moment,
Almost you are not frightened.

But at heart you are frightened, you always have been.

O Pug, obstinate old nervous breakdown,
In the midst of *so* much love,
And such comfort,
Still to feel unsafe and be afraid,

How one's heart goes out to you!

STEVIE SMITH

Erica Thirl's Dog

My nose is wet and shiny, and I never clean my teeth,
Sometime I lie upon my back and show my underneath,
I do things on the pavement when I'm taken to the shops,
And instead of being punished, I am given chocolate drops.

My name is 'Sit', I think, although it might be 'Fetch' or 'Stay',
But whatever people call me I come running anyway,
And I live with Mrs Thirl in quiet South Coastal widowhood,
And we walk and talk together while she throws me bits of
wood.

Sometimes she thinks that I can understand each single word;
I can't. That's why I never find her chattering absurd.
I cannot reason, cannot laugh, I cannot count to ten;
I count one, and then more-than-one, then more-than-one
    again.
Yet people in their more-than-ones to pets like me will turn
For friendship and companionship – both words I cannot learn –
For my conditioned reflexes are just designed to fill
The gap that's left by humans when they're absent, cross or ill.

I never see why I'm considered Mrs Thirl's best friend,
Until her daughter Lynne brings all her brood for the weekend.
Then Mrs Thirl from dawn to dusk makes orange juice and
    cake,
And Lynne says she stays with Don only for the children's sake.
And Mrs Thirl says, 'Darling, your Dad was just the same.
Children, run out in the garden, Gran's too busy for a game.'
Then Lynne goes boo-hoo-hoo and says that next time will be
    final,
And as they cry I lick their salty tears from off the vinyl.

My life's not complicated like the humans she adores,
I don't complain of migraine, or go through the dogopause,
I don't forget to thank her for my birthday postal order,
I never kick my football into her herbaceous border.
I cannot help but wag my tail and pant apparent thanks
(I've no alternative – I'm thick as more-than-one short planks),
But my wagging, and my panting, and my dying-for-the-queen
Is the nearest thing to true love Mrs Thirl has ever seen.

RICHARD STILGOE

The Little Dog from Nowhere

Old Charlie had no friend
And he lived the other end
Of Main Street in a tumbledown old shed.

It was very nearly dark
When he heard a sudden bark
From a little dog from nowhere by his bed.

He was lost and he was tired.
He was hungry, he was scared,
Just a little dog from nowhere in the dark.

He had seen a gleam of light,
Like an opening in the night,
From a tumbledown old shed outside the park.

Old Charlie, all alone,
Gave the little dog a bone;
Took him in and let him lie upon a sack.

As he came in from the cold,
All the night was sudden gold,
For the little dog from nowhere in the shack.

Now Charlie swindled folks galore,
With every other breath, he swore.
He'd con each man or woman he could find.

He cheated all the way
With petty crimes each day.
They said he'd take a shilling from the blind!

And the folks – they used to shun him,
Look right through him, or above him,
Till the little dog from nowhere came around.

Charles was dirty, he was cheap,
He was nothing but a creep.
He had lost all self-respect, so it would seem.

But he was all that mattered
To the little dog that pattered
And followed him as if he were a dream.

With his little head held high,
And his tail towards the sky,
It would follow him as if he were a king.

Every morning they would pass
Through the fragrant meadow-grass,
And the folks who saw forgave him everything.

And I guess that here's a story
With a wealth of hidden glory.
Folk came to know the two of them as one.

And in the end what counted
Was a real respect that mounted
– That the little dog from nowhere had begun.

When they saw him on the street,
All the folks would turn and greet him.
'Mornin' Charlie!' 'Howya, Charlie?' they would cry.

For the man without a friend
– He had found one in the end
– In a little dog from nowhere walking high.

DEREK NEVILLE

The White Rabbit

One white ear up,
One white ear down,
She nuzzles the wire
To be fed;
Sorrel she'll eat,
And burdock-leaves,
And cauliflower-stumps,
And bread;
But when all the nibbling
And twitching is done,
She settles back
On her straw;
For a rabbit likes
To squat in a hutch,
Not thinking much,
If at all.

That's how she behaves in company;
But what does she do when alone?
Has she sprightlier habits? Have tame white rabbits
A friskiness all their own?

Danny crept out
In dark of night,
When the grass was thick
With dew:
He scrabbled the wire
With his finger-nail,
And pushed a green
Leaf through;
But she would not stir
From her sleeping-end,
Nor rouse to his
Whispered call;

For a rabbit's life
Is to squat in a hutch,
Not thinking much,
If at all.

JOHN WALSH

Familiarity Dangerous

As in her ancient mistress' lap,
   The youthful tabby lay,
They gave each other many a tap,
   Alike dispos'd to play.

But strife ensues. Puss waxes warm,
   And with protruded claws
Ploughs all the length of Lydia's arm,
   Mere wantonness the cause.

At once, resentful of the deed,
   She shakes her to the ground
With many a threat, that she shall bleed
   With still a deeper wound.

But, Lydia, bid thy fury rest!
   It was a venial stroke;
For she, that will with kittens jest,
   Should bear a kitten's joke.

WILLIAM COWPER
(translated from the Latin of Vincent Bourne)

Death of a Cat

I rose early
On the fourth day
Of his illness
And went downstairs
To see if he was
All right.

He was not in the
House, and I rushed
Wildly round the
Garden calling his name.

I found him lying
Under a rhododendron
Bush,
His black fur
Wet, and matted
With the dew.

I knelt down beside him
And he opened his
Mouth as if to
Miaow
But no sound came.

I picked him up
And he lay quietly
In my arms
As I carried him
Indoors.

Suddenly he gave
A quiet miaow
And I felt his body tense
And then lie still.

I laid his warm
Lifeless body on
The floor, and
Rubbed my fingers
Through his fur.

A warm tear
Dribbled down
My cheek and
Left a salt taste
On my lips.

I stood up, and
Walked quietly
Out of the room.

ANTHONY THOMPSON

Elegy on the Death of Juliet's Owl

Juliet has lost her little downy owl,
The bird she loved more than all other birds.
He was a darling bird, so white, so wise,
Like a monk hooded in a snowy cowl,
With sun-shy scholar's eyes;
He hooted softly in diminished thirds;
And when he asked for mice,
He took refusal with a silent pride –
And never pleaded twice.
He was a wondrous bird, as dignified
As any Diplomat
That ever sat
By the round table of a Conference.

He was delicious, lovable and soft.
He understood the meaning of the night,
And read the riddle of the smiling stars.
When he took flight,
And roosted high aloft,
Beyond the shrubbery and the garden fence,
He would return and seek his safer bars,
All of his own accord; and he would plead
Forgiveness for the trouble and the search,
And for the anxious heart he caused to bleed,
And settle once again upon his perch,
And utter a propitiating note,
And take the heart
Of Juliet by his pretty winning ways.

His was the art
Of pleasing without effort easily.
His fluffy throat, his sage round eye,
Sad with old knowledge, bright with young amaze,
Where are they now? ah, where?
Perchance in the pale halls of Hecate,
Or in the poplars of Elysium,
He wanders careless and completely free.
But in the regions dumb,
And in the pallid air,
He will not find a sweet caressing hand
Like Juliet's; nor in all that glimmering land
Shall he behold a silver planet rise
As splendid as the light in Juliet's eyes.
Therefore, in weeping with you, Juliet,
Oh! let us not forget,
To drop with sprigs of rosemary and rue,
A not untimely tear
Upon the bier,
Of him who lost so much in losing you.

MAURICE BARING

A Stern Story

I have a little puppy, and he often runs around
　　And tries to catch the tail he hasn't got;
He always seems surprised and hurt to see it can't be found,
　　But knowing men assure me he is not.
Because he was so little that his baby eyes were shut,
　　He never saw it, so he never knew
How very nice and long it was before they had it cut,
　　And only left him just an inch or two.

They say he looks more handsome and is saved a lot of woes;
　　One can't step on a tail that is no more;
Hot cinders cannot burn it, and, as every Manx cat knows,
　　It can't get caught within a slamming door.

But he quivers with excitement from his head down to his toes
    When I light back from the station with my bag,
And he wriggles from his little stump right to his little nose,
    And I *know* he'd like a longer tail to wag.

To My Dog

This gentle beast
This golden beast
laid her long chin
along my wrist

and my wrist
is branded
with her love
and trust

and the salt of my cheek
is hers to lick
so long as I
or she shall last

ADRIAN MITCHELL

The Canary

Mary had a little bird,
  With feathers bright and yellow,
Slender legs – upon my word,
  He was a pretty fellow!

Sweetest notes he always sung,
  Which much delighted Mary;
Often where his cage was hung,
  She sat to hear Canary.

Crumbs of bread and dainty seeds
  She carried to him daily,
Seeking for the early weeds,
  She decked his palace gaily.

This, my little readers, learn,
  And ever practise duly;
Songs and smiles of love return
  To friends who love you truly.

ELIZABETH TURNER

Full Circle

When John was ten they gave the boy
(A farmer's son) no passing toy,
But his own sheep-dog, eight weeks old.
They'd play round barn and rick and fold
Till running, John would turn to find
His puppy sitting far behind.
With puzzled look and whimpers he
Would plead, 'O master, wait for me!'

The years sped on. Through wind and weather
The boy and dog grew up together.
On hill and dale, through heath and fern,
Nor did John need to slow and turn.
When rounding sheep the dog roamed wide
Outstripping far his master's stride;
He'd work the flock, his joy – his pride –
With whistles only as a guide.

And twelve years on the dog was still
A close companion on the hill,
But in the truck he'd often stay
And guard the gear. Now growing grey
In cheek and muzzle, when again
They strolled together down the lane,
He'd pant and pause, and sightless he
Would plead, 'O master, wait for me!'

RUTH SKILLING

My Dog Tray

On the green banks of Shannon when Sheelah was nigh,
No blithe Irish lad was so happy as I;
No harp like my own could so cheerily play,
And wherever I went was my poor dog Tray.

When at last I was forced from my Sheelah to part,
She said, (while the sorrow was big at her heart,)
Oh! remember your Sheelah when far, far away:
And be kind, my dear Pat, to our poor dog Tray.

Poor dog! he was faithful and kind to be sure,
And he constantly loved me although I was poor;
When the sour-looking folk sent me heartless away,
I had always a friend in my poor dog Tray.

When the road was so dark, and the night was so cold,
And Pat and his dog were grown weary and old,
How snugly we slept in my old coat of grey,
And he licked me for kindness – my old dog Tray.

Though my wallet was scant I remembered his case,
Nor refused my last crust to his pitiful face;
But he died at my feet on a cold winter day,
And I played a sad lament for my poor dog Tray.

Where now shall I go, poor, forsaken, and blind?
Can I find one to guide me, so faithful and kind?
To my sweet native village, so far, far away,
I can never more return with my poor dog Tray.

THOMAS CAMPBELL

Robert Herrick's Pig

'A runt, a diddler, that is what you are.'
So said my greedy brothers and my sisters,
Shouldering me away from mother's paps,
As she lay sweet in straw, a beatific grin
Upon her mug, showing her ivory tusks.

They all ended up as chops and sausages,
As bacon and as brawn and as black puddings,
As tripe and chitterlings.
But parson took me in and made me free
Of parlour, hall and kitchen. A sweetling pig,
A nestling pig, a pretty tantony –
That is what I am.

My friend, the parson, is a learned man,
And I a most accomplished pig, for I've been taught
To swill my ale out of a pewter tankard,
While he sits evenings over his wine and dreams
Of youth, and London, and those Mermaid days
When midnight's chimes ring dizzy in our heads
He squeals his little songs to Julia,
And other possibly existent ladies,
And I join with him in the accompaniment –

Hunk hunk hunk snortle snortle snortle snortle
Gruntle gruntle gruntle, wee wee wee wee!

JOHN HEATH-STUBBS

To a Black Greyhound

Shining black in the shining light,
   Inky black in the golden sun,
Graceful as the swallow's flight,
   Light as swallow, wingèd one,
Swift as driven hurricane –
   Double-sinewed stretch and spring,
Muffled thud of flying feet,
   See the black dog galloping,
   Hear his wild foot-beat.

See him lie when the day is dead,
   Black curves curled on the boarded floor.
Sleepy eyes, my sleepy-head –
   Eyes that were aflame before.
Gentle now, they burn no more;
   Gentle now and softly warm,
With the fire that made them bright
   Hidden – as when after storm
   Softly falls the night.

God of speed, who makes the fire –
   God of Peace, who lulls the same –
God who gives the fierce desire,
   Lust for blood as fierce as flame –
God who stands in Pity's name –
   Many may ye be or less,
Ye who rule the earth and sun:
   Gods of strength and gentleness,
   Ye are ever one.

JULIAN GRENFELL

Man and Dog

Who's this – alone with stone and sky?
It's only my old dog and I –
It's only him; it's only me;
Alone with stone and grass and tree.

What share we most – we two together?
Smells, and awareness of the weather.
What is it makes us more than dust?
My trust in him; in me his trust.

Here's anyhow one decent thing
That life to man and dog can bring;
One decent thing, remultiplied
Till earth's last dog and man have died.

SIEGFRIED SASSOON

Inside

A bellyfull and the fire,
And him in his old suit,
And me with my heart's desire,
My head across his foot.

And I doze. And he reads.
And the clock ticks slow.
And, though he never heeds,
He knows, and I know.

Presently, without look,
His hand will feel to tug
My ear, his eyes on book,
Mine upon the rug.

ELEANOR FARJEON

Forgiven

I found a little beetle, so that Beetle was his name,
And I called him Alexander and he answered just the same.
I put him in a match-box, and I kept him all the day . . .
And Nanny let my beetle out –
   Yes, Nanny let my beetle out –
      She went and let my beetle out –
         And Beetle ran away.

She said she didn't mean it, and I never said she did,
She said she wanted matches and she just took off the lid,
She said that she was sorry, but it's difficult to catch
An excited sort of beetle you've mistaken for a match.

She said that she was sorry, and I really mustn't mind,
As there's lot and lots of beetles which she's certain we could
  find
If we looked about the garden for the holes where beetles hid –
And we'd get another beetle and write BEETLE on the lid.

We went to all the places which a beetle might be near
And we made the sort of noises that a beetle likes to hear,
And I saw a kind of something and I gave a sort of shout:
'A beetle-house and Alexander Beetle coming out!'

It was Alexander Beetle I'm as certain as can be,
And he had a sort of look as if he thought it might be Me,
And he had a sort of look as if he thought he ought to say:
'I'm very very sorry that I tried to run away.'

And Nanny's very sorry too for you-know-what-she-did
And she's writing ALEXANDER very blackly on the lid.
So Nan and Me are friends because it's difficult to catch
An excited Alexander you've mistaken for a match.

A. A. MILNE

On the Death of a Cat, Friend of Mine Aged Ten Years and a Half

Who shall tell the lady's grief
When her cat was past relief?
Who shall number the hot tears
Shed o'er her, belov'd for years?
Who shall say the dark dismay
Which her dying caused that day?

Of a noble race she came,
And Grimalkin was her name.
Young and old full many a mouse
Felt the prowess of her house;
Weak and strong full many a rat
Cowered beneath her crushing pat;
And the birds around the place
Shrank from her too-close embrace.
But one night, reft of her strength,
She lay down and died at length:
Lay a kitten by her side
In whose life the mother died.
Spare her life and lineage,
Guard her kitten's tender age,
And that kitten's name as wide
Shall be known as hers that died.
And whoever passes by
The poor grave where Puss doth lie,
Softly, softly let him tread,
Nor disturb her narrow bed.

CHRISTINA ROSSETTI

Nodding

Tizdal my beautiful cat
Lies on the old rag mat
In front of the kitchen fire.
Outside the night is black.

The great fat cat
Lies with his paws under him
His whiskers twitch in a dream,
He is slumbering.

The clock on the mantelpiece
Ticks unevenly, tic-toc, tic-toc,
Good heavens what is the matter
With the kitchen clock?

Outside an owl hunts,
Hee hee hee hee,
Hunting in the Old Park
From his snowy tree.
What on earth can he find in the park tonight,
It is so wintry?

Now the fire burns suddenly too hot
Tizdal gets up to move,
Why should such an animal
Provoke our love?

The twigs from the elder bush
Are tapping on the window pane
As the wind sets them tapping,
Now the tapping begins again.

One laughs on a night like this
In a room half firelight half dark
With a great lump of a cat
Moving on the hearth,
And the twigs tapping quick,
And the owl in an absolute fit
One laughs supposing creation
Pays for its long plodding
Simply by coming to this –
Cat, night, fire – and a girl nodding.

STEVIE SMITH

To a Siamese Cat

I shall walk in the sun alone
Whose golden light you loved:
I shall sleep alone
And stirring touch an empty place:
I shall write uninterrupted –
I would that your gentle paw
Could stay my moving pen just once again!

I shall see beauty,
But none to match your living grace:
I shall hear music,
But not so sweet as the droning song
With which you loved me.

    I shall fill my days,
    But I shall not, cannot forget:
    Sleep soft, dear friend,
    For while I live, you shall not die.

MICHAEL JOSEPH

My Old Cat

My old cat is dead
Who would butt me with his head.
He had the sleekest fur,
He had the blackest purr.
Always gentle with us
Was this black puss,
But when I found him today
Stiff and cold where he lay,
His look was a lion's,
Full of rage, defiance:
O! he would not pretend
That what came was a friend
But met it in pure hate.
Well died, my old cat.

HAL SUMMERS

My Tortoise

I had a sweet tortoise called Pye
Wabbit.
He ate dandelions, it was
His habbit.
Pye Wabbit, Pye Wy-et,
It was more than a habit, it was
His diet.
All the hot summer days, Pye
Wy-et, Pye Wiked-it,
Ate dandelions. I lay on the grass flat to see
How much he liked it.
In the autumn when it got cold, Pye Wiked-it, Pye
Wy-bernator,
Went to sleep till next Spring. He was
a hibernator.
First he made a secret bed for the winter,
To lie there.
We loved him far too much ever
To spy where.
Why does his second name change every time?
Why, to make the rhyme.
Pye our dear tortoise
Is dead and gone.
He lies in the tomb we built for him, called
'Pye's Home',
Pye, our dear tortoise,
We loved him so much.
Is he as dear to you now
As he was to us?

STEVIE SMITH

The Golden Cat

My golden cat has dappled sides;
No prince has worn so fine a cloak
Patterned like sea-water where rides
The sun, or like the flower in oak
When the rough plank has been planed out,
Lovely as yellow mackerel skies
In moonlight, or a speckled trout.
Clear as swung honey were his eyes.

It was a wondrous daily thing
To look for, when his beautiful
Curved body gathered for a spring
That, light as any golden gull,
Flashed over the fine net of wire
Which my casement-window bars;
His leap was bright as tongues of fire,
And swift as autumn shooting-stars.

My cat was like a golden gift,
A golden myth of Grecian lore –
But things so bright, and things so swift,
Must vanish; and he is no more.

ELEANOR FARJEON

A Popular Personage at Home

'I live here: "Wessex" is my name:
I am a dog known rather well:
I guard the house; but how that came
To be my whim I cannot tell.

'With a leap and a heart elate I go
At the end of an hour's expectancy
To take a walk of a mile or so
With the folk I let live here with me.

'Along the path, amid the grass
I sniff, and find out rarest smells
For rolling over as I pass
The open fields towards the dells.

'No doubt I shall always cross this sill,
And turn the corner, and stand steady,
Gazing back for my mistress till
She reaches where I have run already,

'And that this meadow with its brook,
And bulrush, even as it appears
As I plunge by with hasty look,
Will stay the same a thousand years.'

Thus 'Wessex'. But a dubious ray
At times informs his steadfast eye,
Just for a trice, as though to say,
'Yet, will this pass, and pass shall I?'

THOMAS HARDY

Dead 'Wessex' the Dog
to the Household

Do you think of me at all,
    Wistful ones?
Do you think of me at all
    As if nigh?
Do you think of me at all
At the creep of evenfall,
Or when the skybirds call
    As they fly?

Do you look for me at times
    Wistful ones?
Do you look for me at times
    Strained and still?
Do you look for me at times
When the hour for walking chimes,
On that grassy path that climbs
    Up the hill?

You may hear a jump or trot,
    Wistful ones,
You may hear a jump or trot –
    Mine, as 'twere –
You may hear a jump or trot
On the stair or path or plot;
But I shall cause it not,
    Be not there.

Should you call as when I knew you,
　　Wistful ones,
Should you call as when I knew you,
　　Shared your home;
Should you call as when I knew you,
I shall not turn to view you,
I shall not listen to you,
　　Shall not come.

THOMAS HARDY

Epitaph

What is this stone he's laid upon my bones,
For whom I fetched and carried endless stones?
Wait, Master, wait a little. When we meet
You'll know me by my stone, laid at your feet.

ELEANOR FARJEON

NIGHT'S LIVING THINGS

The Bat

The beggarly Bat, a cut out, scattily
Begs at the lamp's light
A bright moth-mote.

What wraps his shivers?
Scraps of moon cloth
Snatched off cold rivers.

Scissored bits
Of the moon's fashion-crazes
Are his disguises
And wrap up his fits –

For the jittery bat's
Determined to burst
Into day, like the sun

But he never gets past
The dawn's black posts.

As long as night lasts
The shuttlecock Bat
Is battered about
By the rackets of ghosts.

TED HUGHES

The Bat

Myself, I rather like the bat,
It's not a mouse, it's not a rat.
It has no feathers, yet has wings,
It's quite inaudible when it sings.
It zigzags through the evening air
And never lands on ladies' hair,
A fact of which men spend their lives
Attempting to convince their wives.

OGDEN NASH

The Bat

By day the bat is cousin to the mouse.
He likes the attic of an aging house.

His fingers make a hat about his head.
His pulse beat is so slow we think him dead.

He loops in crazy figures half the night
Among the trees that face the corner light.
But when he brushes up against a screen,
We are afraid of what our eyes have seen;

For something is amiss or out of place
When mice with wings can wear a human face.

THEODORE ROETHKE

Bats

A bat is born
Naked and blind and pale.
His mother makes a pocket of her tail
And catches him. He clings to her long fur
By his thumbs and toes and teeth.
And then the mother dances through the night
Doubling and looping, soaring, somersaulting –
Her baby hangs on underneath.
All night, in happiness, she hunts and flies.
Her high sharp cries
Like shining needlepoints of sound
Go out into the night and, echoing back,

Tell her what they have touched.
She hears how far it is, how big it is,
Which way it's going:
She lives by hearing.
The mother eats the moths and gnats she catches
In full flight; in full flight
The mother drinks the water of the pond
She skims across. Her baby hangs on tight.
Her baby drinks the milk she makes him
In moonlight or starlight, in mid-air.
Their single shadow, printed on the moon
Or fluttering across the stars,
Whirls on all night; at daybreak
The tired mother flaps home to her rafter.
The others all are there.

They hang themselves up by their toes,
They wrap themselves in their brown wings.
Bunched upside-down, they sleep in air.
Their sharp ears, their sharp teeth, their quick sharp faces
Are dull and slow and mild.
All the bright day, as the mother sleeps,
She folds her wings about her sleeping child.

RANDALL JARRELL

The Badgers

Brocks snuffle from their holt within
A writhen root of black-thorn old,
And moonlight streaks the gashes bold
Of lemon fur from ear to chin.
They stretch and snort and snuff the air,
Then sit to plan the night's affair.

The neighbours, fox and owl, they heed,
And many whispering scents and sounds
Familiar on their secret rounds,
Then silently make sudden speed,
Paddling away in single file
Adown the eagle fern's dim aisle.

EDEN PHILPOTTS

Badger

I wait in my fear at the edge of the wood,
the evening mild, the round moon
rising bland over the familiar hill.
All day I drowsed in the warm sett,
curled up in troubled dream
on matted grass and fern,
the silver cubs gone,
not daring to come out for the night walk.
And she, hanging dead and alone,
upside down on the spiked wire,
badge streaked with old blood,
torn flesh fermenting round smashed skull.

I heard her scream to the deaf stars,
brute cudgels beating the small life out,
her agony into my ears,
the red-eyed torches deceiving the dark,
dry leaves crackling beneath enemy feet.
I shiver here in my lonely fur, lift
my nose high for betraying scent,
find none, shuffle back home,
not wishing to play, roll by myself
along the moon's path, head-over-heels.
Her glassy eyes seem to search me out,
but must go on, groping for roots, snails,
keep company with wasp grubs,
spring-clean when the weather turns,
her bones picked white in murdered air.

LEONARD CLARK

Dear Brother Horse

I woke. Without, the full moon's light
Lay on the stubble white as snow,
And still and bare as far-off wastes
Where anxious travellers go.

Beyond them lay the gilded sea,
Unmoved by wave or swell,
A lighthouse shone on vacancy
And mutely signalled, 'All is well'.

There was no sound, nor wind nor bird
Brought life to the enchanted night;
Until all suddenly he came
As if created out of light:

Created out of light, as swift –
He leaped the wheatfield's border rail,
A horse escaped from Master Man,
Proud head raised high, and banner tail;

Then paused – I worshipped Beauty there,
For all Life's loveliness was he,
Before he snorted, and was gone,
And left the empty night to me.

WALTER DE LA MARE

Two Pewits

Under the after-sunset sky
Two pewits sport and cry,
More white than is the moon on high
Riding the dark surge silently;

More black than earth. Their cry
Is the one sound under the sky.
They alone move, now low, now high,
And merrily they cry
To the mischievous Spring sky,
Plunging earthward, tossing high,
Over the ghost who wonders why
So merrily they cry and fly,
Nor choose 'twixt earth and sky,
While the moon's quarter silently
Rides, and earth rests as silently.

EDWARD THOMAS

Hares at Play

The birds are gone to bed, the cows are still,
And sheep lie panting on each old mole-hill;
And underneath the willow's grey-green bough,
Like toil a-resting, lies the fallow plough.
The timid hares throw daylight fears away
On the lane's road to dust and dance and play,
Then dabble in the grain by naught deterred
To lick the dew-fall from the barley's beard;
Then out they sturt again and round the hill
Like happy thoughts dance, squat, and loiter still,
Till milking maidens in the early morn
Jingle their yokes and sturt them in the corn;
Through well-known beaten paths each nimbling hare
Sturts quick as fear, and seeks its hidden lair.

JOHN CLARE

Night Walk

What are you doing away up there
On your great long legs in the lonely air?
  Come down here, where the scents are sweet,
  Swirling around your great, wide feet.

How can you know of the urgent grass
And the whiff of the wind that will whisper and pass
  Or the lure of the dark of the garden hedge
  Or the trail of a cat on the road's black edge?

What are you doing away up there
On your great long legs in the lonely air?
  You miss so much at your great, great height
  When the ground is full of the smells of night.

Hurry then, quickly, and slacken my lead
For the mysteries speak and the messages speed
  With the talking stick and the stone's slow mirth
  That four feet find on the secret earth.

MAX FATCHEN

from *The Glow-worm*

Beneath the hedge or near the stream
  A worm is known to stray,
That shows by night a lucid beam
  Which disappears by day.

Disputes have been, and still prevail
  From whence his rays proceed;
Some give that honour to his tail.
  And others to his head.

But this is sure – the hand of night
  That kindles up the skies,
Gives him a modicum of light
  Proportioned to his size.

Perhaps indulgent nature meant,
  By such a lamp bestowed,
To bid the traveller, as he went,
  Be careful where he trod.

Nor crush a worm, whose useful light
     Might serve, however small,
To show a stumbling stone by night,
     And save him from a fall ...

WILLIAM COWPER
(translated from the Latin of Vincent Bourne)

The Moth

Isled in the midnight air,
Musked with the dark's faint bloom,
Out into glooming and secret haunts
     The flame cries, 'Come!'

Lovely in dye and fan,
A-tremble in shimmering grace,
A moth from her winter swoon
     Uplifts her face:

Stares from her glamorous eyes;
Wafts her on plumes like mist;
In ecstasy swirls and sways
     To her strange tryst.

WALTER DE LA MARE

Lunar Moth

From the forest of night
Cometh the light
Green-wingèd flight –

Titania* come
To a mortal's home
From the low-moon land
With her wings and her wand
And her bright black eyes
And her tiny feet
And her wings pale green
Like wind through wheat.
Now I am wise,
For now I have seen
Men told no lies
Of a fairy queen.
She was here on the wall,
And now she has gone,
Quiet, small,
To the night, alone.
With a wave of her wand
She vanished, beyond
The sky to the cool
Moon of July.

ROBERT HILLYER

* Titania: Queen of the Fairies.

Barn Owl

Round owl,
round and white
with moonglass eyes
a cry of fright in the wood
where movement dies.
Then windless, milky flight
in search of blood.

Stone owl,
still as stone
struck from Minerva's shield
in hayloft hole,
watching through daylight-shuttered eyes
till darkness fold
in sleep the unsleeping field.

Round owl ringed in a world alone.

PHOEBE HESKETH

Dusk

This is the owl moment I have always known,
Not yet completely dark,
When small birds twit him in the park,
In terror though they tease.
Out he comes among the trees,
He comes on oiled wings, alone,
And mice and tucked-up children hear
His long too-whoo as old as fear.

FRANCES CORNFORD

The Spun-gold Fox

Sing in the silver fog of night,
Voice of a fox-hound, bellow bright,
Sing me the silver song of fox,
Wary and watching the moon-dipped rocks.

Quivering nostril, lifted paw,
Sniffing the mist for the smell of dog.
Sing me fox-hound, lemon-white,
Sing me the song of a fox tonight.
Bay me the story, old, old, old,
Of a fox that runs and a moon that's cold;
In the valley, the hill, near the speckled rocks
Bay me the run of the spun-gold fox.

PATRICIA HUBBELL

Fox

Who
Wears the smartest evening dress in England?
Checks his watch by the stars
And hurries, white-scarfed,
To the opera
In the flea-ridden hen-house
Where he will conduct the orchestra?

Who
With a Robin Hood mask over his eyes
Meets King Pheasant the Magnificent
And with silent laughter
Shakes all the gold out of his robes
Then carries him bodily home
Over his shoulder,
A swag-bag?

And who
Flinging back his Dracula cloak
And letting one fang wink in the moonlight
Lifts off his top hat

Shows us the moon through the bottom of it
Then brings out of it, in a flourish of feathers,
The gander we locked up at sunset?

TED HUGHES

Hedgehog

Twitching the leaves just where the drainpipe clogs
In ivy leaves and mud, a purposeful
Creature at night about its business. Dogs
Fear his stiff seriousness. He chews away

At beetles, worms, slugs, frogs. Can kill a hen
With one snap of his jaws, can taunt a snake
To death on muscled spines. Old countrymen
Tell tales of hedgehogs sucking a cow dry.

But this one, cramped by houses, fences, walls,
Must have slept here all winter in that heap
Of compost, or have inched by intervals
Through tidy gardens to this ivy bed.

And here, dim-eyed, but ears so sensitive
A voice within the house can make him freeze,
He scuffs the edge of danger, yet can live
Happily in our nights and absences.

A country creature, wary, quiet and shrewd,
He takes the milk we give him, when we're gone.
At night, our slamming voices must seem crude
To one who sits and waits for silences.

ANTHONY THWAITE

The Composition

'A hedgehog is a creature with four legs, and thorns.'
That's what the roadman said,
So when I found one ambling uncertainly
On ridiculous, small feet, along the way
That's lined with dandelions and deadnettles
I thought: 'There's a hedgehog!
I wonder if he'll stay?'

We put out milk in a saucer.
Night by night
It disappeared. But we never saw him take it
Until once I came down swiftly
In pyjamas
Treading on each stair carefully –
Not to creak it –

And there he was, not alone, but with a trickle
Of wife and children wobbling after him
Scuffling their feet in the dark, wet grass.
I watched them
Nuzzling and snuffling at the saucer's brim
With a soft, sweet, sucking sound . . .

Next time I pass
Near the cinderpath with the dandelions
I shall look
For a creature with four legs, and thorns growing on it,
Wambling along like a hedge with no rose in it.
I might even write about him
In a book.

JEAN KENWARD

The Lark

There is a small bird cowering in the dark;
His wing is broken, he will no more sing;
He will not fly, nor sing again, the lark
With a broken wing!

The bird that cowers with a broken wing
Is all alone – His mate has gone away:
In the morrow, in the sun, in the field, his mate will sing
Her wonted lay.

In the dew, in the limpid dawn, in the ray
Of the sun, she'll sing the comrade gone
Who will not cheer a sunny day
Again for anyone.

All panic looks and listens with his eyes!
He is all fear! He is no more a lark!
Only the heart dares stir of him that lies
In the dark.

JAMES STEPHENS

Tick-a-Lick

Tick-a-lick cat time,
Paw lick, ear lick, whiskers.
Tick-a-lick tale flick,
Fur time, feather time,
Leaves scuffle, time shuttle,
Mouse house, cheese fleas,
Scratch thatch,
Open fire, cowbyre.

Tick-a-lick lap time,
Saucer lick, bowl lick, whiskers.
White, milk, drops.
Tick-a-lick sleep time,
Stretch out, claws out,
Fire's out.

Tick-a-night crouch time,
Pounce it, crunched it, whiskers.
Tick-a-night witches,
Broom-stick, moon-tricks,
Trouble bubble, prickly stubble,
Screech, retch,
Hallowe'en
Midnight.

Tick-a-lick moon's out,
Stars out, fire's out.
Tick-a-day night's out.
Tick-a-lick a
Tick-a-lick-
a tick-
a

RONA M. CAMPBELL

The Cat and the Moon

The cat went here and there
And the moon spun round like a top,
And the nearest kin of the moon,
The creeping cat, looked up.
Black Minnaloushe stared at the moon,
For, wander and wail as he would,
The pure cold light in the sky
Troubled his animal blood.
Minnaloushe runs in the grass
Lifting his delicate feet.
Do you dance, Minnaloushe, do you dance?
When two close kindred meet,
What better than call a dance?
Maybe the moon may learn,
Tired of that courtly fashion,
A new dance turn.
Minnaloushe creeps through the grass
From moonlit place to place,
The sacred moon overhead
Has taken a new phase.
Does Minnaloushe know that his pupils
Will pass from change to change,
And that from round to crescent,
From crescent to round they range?
Minnaloushe creeps through the grass
Alone, important and wise,
And lifts to the changing moon
His changing eyes.

W. B. YEATS

That Cat

The cat that comes to my window sill
When the moon looks cold and the night is still —
He comes in a frenzied state alone
With a tail that stands like a pine tree cone,
And says: 'I have finished my evening lark,
And I think I can hear a hound dog bark.
My whiskers are froze and stuck to my chin.
I do wish you'd git up and let me in.'
   That cat gits in.

But if in the solitude of the night
He doesn't appear to be feeling right,
And rises and stretches and seeks the floor,
And some remote corner he would explore,
And doesn't feel satisfied just because
There's no good spot for to sharpen his claws,
And meows and canters uneasy about
Beyond the least shadow of any doubt
   That cat gits out.

BEN KING

The Rabbits' Song Outside the Tavern

We, who play under the pines,
We, who dance in the snow
That shines blue in the light of the moon,
Sometimes halt as we go –

Stand with our ears erect,
Our noses testing the air,
To gaze at the golden world
Behind the windows there.

Suns they have in a cave,
Stars, each on a tall white stem,
And the thought of a fox or an owl
Seems never to trouble them.
They laugh and eat and are warm,
Their food is ready at hand,
While hungry out in the cold
We little rabbits stand.

But they never dance as we dance!
They haven't the speed or the grace.
We scorn both the dog and the cat
Who lie by their fireplace.
We scorn them licking their paws
Their eyes on an upraised spoon –
We who dance hungry and wild
Under a winter's moon.

ELIZABETH COATSWORTH

Master Rabbit

As I was walking,
Thyme sweet to my nose,
Green grasshoppers talking,
Rose rivalling rose:

Wings clear as amber,
Outspread in the light,
As from bush to bush
The Linnet took flight:

Master Rabbit I saw
In the shadow-rimmed mouth
Of his sandy cavern
Looking out to the South.

'Twas dew-tide coming,
The turf was sweet
To nostril, curved tooth,
And wool-soft feet.

Sun was in West,
Crystal in beam
Of its golden shower
Did his round eye gleam.

Lank horror was I,
And a foe, poor soul –
Snowy flit of a scut,
He was into his hole:

And – *stamp, stamp, stamp*
Through dim labyrinths clear –
The whole world darkened:
A Human near!

WALTER DE LA MARE

The Rabbit

Not even when the early birds
Danced on my roof with showery feet
Such music as will come from rain –
Not even then could I forget
The rabbit in his hours of pain;
Where, lying in an iron trap,
He cries all through the deafened night –
Until his smiling murderer comes,
To kill him in the morning light.

W. H. DAVIES

Hi!

Hi! handsome hunting man
Fire your little gun.
Bang! now the animal
Is dead and dumb and done.
Nevermore to peep again, creep again, leap again,
Eat or sleep or drink again, Oh, what fun!

WALTER DE LA MARE

Done For

Old Ben Bailey
He's been and done
For a small brown bunny
With his long gun.

Glazed are the eyes
That stared so clear,
And no sound stirs
In that hairy ear.

What was once beautiful
Now breathes not,
Bound for Ben Bailey's
Smoking pot.

WALTER DE LA MARE

The Cattle

The quiet-eyed cattle
Are nervous and heavy
They clumsily huddle
And settle together

The mists of their breathing
Are wreathing and twining
And wisp to the window
And fade in the moonlight

Out over the meadow
Where cattle tomorrow
Will amble in pasture
And always remember

Will always remember
The King in their stable
The Child in the manger
Whose name lives forever.

LESLIE NORRIS

Mice in the Hay

out of the lamplight
   whispering worshipping
the mice in the hay

timid eyes pearl-bright
   whispering worshipping
whisking quick and away

they were there that night
   whispering worshipping
smaller than snowflakes are

quietly made their way
   whispering worshipping
close to the manger

yes, they were afraid
   whispering worshipping
as the journey was made

from a dark corner
   whispering worshipping
scuttling together

But He smiled to see them
   whispering worshipping
there in the lamplight

stretched out His hand to them
   they saw the baby King
hurried back out of sight
   whispering worshipping

LESLIE NORRIS

A Manger Song

Whence got ye your soft, soft eyes of the mother, O soft-eyed cow?
We saw the Mother of mothers bring forth, and that was how.
We sheltered her that was shelterless for a little while,
We watched the milking Babe at her breast, and we saw her
    smile.
Even as we she lay upon straw, and even as we
Took her sleep in the dark of the manger unfretfully,
And when the dawn of the strange new Star discovered her thus,
The ray that was destined for her and for Him fell also on us;
The light passed into her eyes and ours, and full in its flood
We were first to behold the first mothering look of the Mother
    of God.

ELEANOR FARJEON

Lullaby for a Baby Toad

Sleep, my child:
The dark dock leaf
Spreads a tent
To hide your grief.
The thing you saw
In the forest pool
When you bent to drink
In the evening cool
Was a mask that He,
The Wisest Toad,
Gave us to hide
Our precious load –
The jewel that shines
In the flat toad-head,
With gracious sapphire
And changing red.

For if, my toadling,
Your face were fair
As the precious jewel
That glimmers there,
Man, the jealous,
Man, the cruel,
Would look at you
And suspect the jewel.

So dry the tears
From your hornèd eyes,
And eat your supper
Of dew and flies;
Curl in the shade
Of the nettles deep,
Think of your jewel
And go to sleep.

STELLA GIBBONS

Index of First Lines

Index of Poets

Acknowledgements

The editor and publishers gratefully acknowledge permission to reproduce copyright poems in this book:

'Elegy on the Death of Juliet's Owl' by Maurice Baring, reprinted by permission of A. P. Watt Ltd on behalf of the Trustees of the Maurice Baring Will Trust; 'Bee' and 'Lamb' by George Barker, reprinted from *The Alphabetical Zoo* by permission of Faber and Faber Ltd; 'Pigeons' by Patricia Beer, reprinted from *The Lie of the Land* by permission of the author and Century Hutchinson Ltd; 'The Fawn in the Snow' by William Rose Benét, reprinted by permission of David Higham Associates Ltd; 'Trouvée' from *Complete Poems* by Elizabeth Bishop. Copyright © 1968 by Elizabeth Bishop, Copyright © 1983 by Alice Helen Methfessel. Originally published in the *New Yorker*. Reprinted by permission of Farrar, Straus and Giroux, Inc.; 'Bumble Bee' by N. M. Bodecker, reprinted from *Snowman Sniffles* by permission of Faber and Faber Ltd; 'Sheep' and 'Horse' by Alan Brownjohn, reprinted by permission of the author; 'Simply a Slug', 'Cow Pâté' and 'Tick-a-Lick' by Rona M. Campbell, reprinted by permission of the author; 'Lark', 'Twins' 'Earth-worm', 'Cock Pheasant', 'Cat in Winter', 'Badger' and 'Three Butterflies' from *Collected Poems and Verses for Children* by Leonard Clark, reprinted by permission of Dobson Books Ltd; 'The Pale Horse' by Leonard Clark from *The Singing Time*, reprinted by permission of Hodder & Stoughton Ltd; 'The Lost Heifer' by Austin Clarke, reprinted by permission of Dolmen Press Ltd; 'The Rabbits' Song outside the Tavern', reprinted by permission of Macmillan Publishing Company from *Away Goes Sally* by Elizabeth Coatsworth. Copyright 1934 by Macmillan Publishing Company, renewed 1962 by Elizabeth Coatsworth Beston; 'A Stern Story' by F. Conquest, reproduced by permission of Punch Publications Ltd; 'Early Waking', 'Country Idyll', 'The Herd', 'A Child's Dream', 'Dusk' and 'To a Young Cat in the Orchard' by Frances Cornford, reprinted by permission of Century Hutchinson Ltd; 'here's a little mouse' by e. e. cummings from *Complete Poems 1913–1962*, reprinted by permission of Liveright Publishing Corporation and of Grafton Books, a division of the Collins Publishing Group; 'Magpies', 'D is for Dog' and 'The Rabbit' by W. H. Davies, reprinted from *The Complete Poems of W. H. Davies* by permission of the Executors of the W. H. Davies Estate and of Jonathan Cape Ltd; 'Snail' by John Drinkwater, reprinted by permission of Sidgwick and Jackson Ltd; 'Rabbits' and 'Birds' by Ray Fabrizio, reprinted by permission of the author; 'Robin's Round' by U. A. Fanthorpe, reprinted by permission of Peterloo Poets; 'K is for Kestrel', 'Inside', 'The Golden Cat', 'Epitaph', 'A Manger Song' and 'A Dragon Fly' by Eleanor Farjeon, reprinted from *Silver Sand and Snow* by permission of David Higham Associates Ltd; 'Night Walk' by Max Fatchen from *Songs for My Dog and Other People*, copyright © 1980 by Max Fatchen, reprinted by permission of Penguin Books Ltd; 'Foul Fowl' by Frank Flynn, copyright © Frank Flynn, 1984. Reprinted from *The Candy-floss Tree*: poems by Gerda Mayer, Frank Flynn and Norman Nicholson (1984) by permission of Oxford University Press; 'Seven Flies' and 'Lonely Horse' from

Rabbit' by John Walsh reprinted from *The Truants* (Heinemann) and 'The New Pullets' by John Walsh from *The Roundabout by the Sea* (Oxford University Press), both by permission of Mrs A. M. Walsh; 'Heaven' from *Upbeat: poems and stories* by Micheline Wandor 1982, reprinted by permission of the Journeyman Press Ltd; 'There's a Toad in the Road at Piccadilly' by John Whitworth reprinted by permission of the author; 'Halfway' by Judith Wright, reprinted from *Collected Poems 1942–1970* with the permission of Angus and Robertson Publishers; 'Our Hamster's Life' by Kit Wright, reprinted from *Rabbitting On* by permission of the author and Collins Publishers; 'The Cat and the Moon' by W. B. Yeats, reprinted from *The Collected Poems of W. B. Yeats* by permission of A. P. Watt Ltd on behalf of Michael B. Yeats and Macmillan London Ltd; 'A Child's Voice', 'A Shot Magpie', 'The Eagle' and 'The Rat' by Andrew Young, reprinted from *The Poetical Works of Andrew Young*, by permission of Martin Secker and Warburg Ltd.

Every effort has been made to trace copyright holders, but in a few cases this has proved impossible. The editor and publishers apologize for these cases of unwilling copyright transgression and would like to hear from any copyright holders not acknowledged.

THE EARTHSICK ASTRONAUT

In this original and exciting collection of children's poems, chosen from entries to the *Observer* National Children's Poetry Competition, the earth is seen through many different eyes.

GARGLING WITH JELLY

Brian Patten

A wonderful collection of poems, mostly funny, one or two serious, but all with something to make the reader think twice.

SKY IN THE PIE

Roger McGough

Brimming with vitality and humour, and spiced with thoughtful observations, this live-wire collection of poems will appeal to every young reader.

SELECTED CAUTIONARY VERSES
Hilaire Belloc

Funny and famous cautionary tales in verse.

THE PUFFIN BOOK OF MAGIC VERSE
ed. Charles Causley

Every kind of magic is reflected in the poems in this splendid anthology.

DUCKS AND DRAGONS
ed. Gene Kemp

Children take to poetry like ducks to water, says Gene Kemp in the introduction to her anthology. A wide variety of poems, all tried and tested in the classroom.

YOU TELL ME
Roger McGough and Michael Rosen

A collection of largely humorous poems by two well-known poets. Sad, funny, serious and zany, they reflect thoughtfully on everyday life.

CUSTARD AND COMPANY
Ogden Nash

A selection of Ogden Nash's humorous verse for children, selected and illustrated profusely by Quentin Blake.

I LIKE THIS POEM
ed. Kaye Webb

A unique collection of poems chosen by children for children. Illustrated by Antony Maitland.